Flames in the Ruins

Other Novels by Gerald Holt

Mystery on the Fen
The Ghostly Tales of Mr. Tooth
Ben and Jacky and the Missing Diamond
Tails of Flame

Flames in the Ruins

Gerald Holt

Order this book online at www.trafford.com
or email orders@trafford.com

Most Trafford titles are also available at major online book retailers.

Printed in the United States of America.

ISBN: 978-1-4269-3382-0 (sc)

*Our mission is to efficiently provide the world's finest, most comprehensive
book publishing service, enabling every author to experience success.
To find out how to publish your book, your way, and have it
available worldwide, visit us online at www.trafford.com*

Trafford rev. 10/07/2010

   www.trafford.com

North America & international
toll-free: 1 888 232 4444 (USA & Canada)
phone: 250 383 6864 ♦ fax: 812 355 4082

CONTENTS

Part 1 – The Ruins

Chapter 1	The Challenge	1
Chapter 2	Black Market	8
Chapter 3	Mines and Mashed Potatoes	15
Chapter 4	A Thief?	20
Chapter 5	Gustav Strasse Sieben	25
Chapter 6	The Camera	32
Chapter 7	Thump! Thump! Thump!	38
Chapter 8	The Fraternizer	45
Chapter 9	Compass Needle	50
Chapter 10	Like Father, like Son	58
Chapter 11	The Escape	66
Chapter 12	To Swim or not to Swim	73
Chapter 13	Fishy Business	80
Chapter 14	A Master for Fishing	84
Chapter 15	Double Summer Time	89
Chapter 16	Peace in our Time	97

Part 2 – The Boy

Chapter 17	A Rickety Old Bicycle	107
Chapter 18	Swimming Lessons	113
Chapter 19	The Nightmare	122
Chapter 20	Two Scrumpers	129

Chapter 21   One Huge Commotion   136
Chapter 22   Peeping Tim   143
Chapter 23   Return of the Wanderer   153

Part 3 – The Grandfather

Chapter 24   Fertilizer   163
Chapter 25   Kundstdünger   169
Chapter 26   Bomber Pilot   173
Chapter 27   Photograph Number Eight   181
Chapter 28   Fritz! Bist du es?   191
Chapter 29   Flames in the Ruins   197
Chapter 30   Silent Night   204

Glossary – German Words and Phrases   **211**

Part 1

THE RUINS

Chapter 1

THE CHALLENGE

Tim stank! The smell was disgusting!

His boots, his socks, his short gray flannel trousers and the sleeves of his dark blue jacket were covered in smelly green-black slime, the stinking slime of rotting grass clippings.

It had started at morning break.

'Hey! You! New boy! Sprog!'

Tim groaned inwardly as he turned to see who was shouting. He knew he was the sprog. It was always the same starting at a new school; someone would challenge the new boy, especially one arriving half way through the summer term as he had done today.

'Think you're too good to talk to us, do you?'

The speaker was the boy who sat immediately behind him in class. He had very short, straight fair hair, shiny and slicked down with hair cream, but despite all the grease a spiky tuft of hair stuck straight up at the back of his head. His pale gray-blue eyes, half closed as he stared at Tim over a large nose, were small and close-set, and his thick lips were thrust out aggressively.

Tim could see that the boy was a bully. He shrugged. 'I thought it was you who didn't want to talk to me.'

He looked at the group gathered round the fair-haired boy. There were about a dozen boys from his class, all around twelve years old. Tim sighed. It was always the same; there was always someone who thought he was kingpin and had to prove it.

The boy stood with feet apart, heavy legs made thicker by long, dark-gray wool socks pulled up high beneath his knees. About ten or twelve fountain pens and propelling pencils were arranged neatly in a gleaming row in the breast pocket of his dark-blue flannel jacket. 'Cheeky with it, eh?' he said, leaning towards Tim.

Some of the boys laughed. One of them said: 'Show him, Welchy. He's a cheeky one alright!'

Tim shrugged. He knew there'd be a challenge of some sort and he wondered what it would be. The fair-haired boy was grinning, looking him up and down. He'd probably have to fight.

'Follow me, sprog!' The boy swung round, his heavy leather boots ringing loudly on the stone flagged floor of the entrance hall as he strode purposefully towards the open doors leading to the school yard.

The other boys closed rank around Tim and he felt himself being hustled forward. 'Might as well get it over with,' he thought. He walked past the heavy dark-stained wooden doors and down the worn stone steps.

'Think you can beat me to those bushes?' The boy pointed. About a hundred yards away, to the side of the main red brick building, were two clumps of bushes. Between them was a narrow gap.

Tim judged the distance. Looking at the heavy-set boy he knew he could beat him. He nodded.

'Right!' The boy looked round. 'McKay! Woods! You, Marchant and Pritchard mark the finish.' He was smiling. 'We'll race to the other side, through the gap.'

The four boys ran off. Tim waited. The remaining boys were sniggering. McKay had reached the bushes. He stopped and walked slowly through the gap. Pritchard followed. The other two stopped and stood on either side of the entry through the bushes.

'You start us, Mugford!'

'Okay, Welchy' A tall, dark haired boy stepped forward. Tim moved to stand next to Welchy.

'Not so close!' Welchy shoved Tim away with his elbow. 'I don't like anyone close.'

Tim moved away and half-crouched.

'On your marks! Get set! Go!'

Before Mugford shouted 'go' Welchy was away and running. Tim was mad. He should have known the bully would cheat. Welchy had a five yard lead, arms pumping up and down, his thick legs thrusting him forward. But Tim was gaining. As Welchy looked back grinning, Tim surged forward and passed him. The bushes were now less than twenty yards away. He ran, straining to open the distance between him and his opponent. He heard his challenger panting heavily behind him. There was the gap. As he burst through he saw McKay and Pritchard fifteen or twenty yards away. They were smiling, waving him on. He smiled back, doubling his effort. Then he felt the ground sink beneath him. There was a terrible cloying smell and he heard Welchy laugh as he sank into muck almost to his waist. He put his hands out to save himself, but all that did was get his hands and the sleeves of his jacket covered in green-black slime. He was in a compost pit, a decaying mass of slimy, dark green rotting grass and blackened leaves.

Tim turned round slowly to look at Welchy, the thick gooey mess clinging, sucking at his legs. The fair-haired boy laughed. 'Hey! New boy! You're not too good now, are you, sprog?'

As Tim struggled up out of the muck the school bell rang for the end of the morning break. Welchy and the others ran off, leaving him to get himself out of the filth in the pit.

'How did this happen?' Mum stood at the foot of the stairs leading down into the basement of their new home. It was one of several houses in a small village named Alstemarschen a few miles outside Hamburg in the British zone of occupied Germany.

'A boy in my class tricked me, Mum. He challenged me to a race. I didn't know there was a compost pit at the end of the course, and no one else told me.'

'Who was this boy?'

'Someone called Welchy, Mum.'

'You must mean young Reggie Welch. He's about your age. He lives just down the road on Schulhaus Strasse. His father's in the CCG.'

'What's that, Mum?'

'Oh, of course, you wouldn't know, Tim. It's the Control Commission for Germany, the CCG. They're the administration group here in the British zone. Your father isn't very fond of Mr. Welch. He's going to be even less happy after this.'

'Why doesn't Dad like him, Mum?'

'I'll leave your father to explain that. Now get those stinking clothes off. Ugh!' Mum waved her hands in front of her face. 'Phew! Just leave them on the floor. How we're going to get them clean I don't know. And your clothes ration book barely has any coupons left.'

Tim started to srip off.

'Leave your underclothes on, Tim and get upstairs. I've asked Inge to run a bath for you.'

Tim was glad that Mum had said to leave his vest and pants on. Mum still seemed to think it was alright for him to be naked when she came into the bathroom, she said she'd seen him like that since he was a baby. But he didn't want to be naked in front of the German maid. He ran up the stairs.

Inge was just coming out of the bathroom, steam seeming to trail behind her in a white cloud. 'A lovely hot bath, Mr. Tim.' When Inge said 'lovely' it sounded like 'loffely'. She smiled.

'Thank you, Inge.' Tim squeezed past the maid and closed the bathroom door. The bath was half full of steaming hot water. He remembered the weekly baths during the war at home in England. Because of rationing there was only enough coal to heat the boiler for baths once a week; and then there was only enough for five inches of water. The rest of the week it was lukewarm water in the sink and a stand-up wash of face, neck, arms and knees. 'And don't forget to do behind your ears!'

Tim smiled as he tested the water with his left big toe before carefully lowering his foot into the bath. The water was just right. Quickly, he removed his underwear, climbed in and lay down, submerging himself up to his chin. It was glorious. He lay there and soaked, then sat up and soaped himself. He lay back again. He heard Sarah come in from school for lunch, and then Dad a minute or two later.

Then, in the distance, he heard an explosion. It sounded like a bomb or a doodlebug exploding. But it couldn't be a bomb! It was May 1947! The war in Europe had been over for two years!

The bath seemed to shudder beneath him and the bathroom door shook. The window rattled and he thought the glass would shatter. Then there was a strange rumbling sound, getting louder and nearer.

Tim grasped the rim of the bath and pushed himself up. In his haste to get out of the bath he slipped on the tile floor. Struggling to his knees he watched wide-eyed as the black rubber stopper from the bath shot up like a bullet through the hot soapy water. It hit the ceiling with such force that it was embedded in the white plaster. A thick snake of oily gray-brown water followed, reaching almost to the ceiling before falling apart. Instinctively Tim ducked just before the dirty water splattered over him and onto the floor. There was an awful smell of rot and decay, ten times worse than the smell of the rotting grass this morning.

Tim's stomach heaved. He couldn't take any more of this. He covered his nose and mouth with the bath towel but the smell was everywhere, thick and heavy. More rumbling came from the pipes and then a gurgling noise as the now filthy bath water seemed to rush to escape down the drain. Tim struggled to get up. The floor was slippery and he fell several times before reaching the door. He could hear Sarah and 'baby' Jane crying and the noise of running feet pounding up the stairs and down the hall. As he grasped the brass handle the door was thrust open and he was pushed back. He tried to keep his balance but his feet slipped from under him and he fell.

Chapter 2

BLACK MARKET

'How do you feel today, Tim?'

Tim forced his eyes open. There was a dull ache, a throbbing pain behind his right ear where he'd hit his head on the bath yesterday. He'd wakened earlier in the morning and carefully felt the egg-sized lump behind his ear. Then he'd closed his eyes trying to shut out the pain. Now, as he moved his head to look up at Dad his brain felt like jelly, thick and heavy inside his skull. But the searing pain from yesterday had faded to a dull ache; the pills the army doctor had given him seemed to be working.

'A little better thanks, Dad. My head still hurts, but it's not half as bad as it was last night.'

'Mm!' Dad nodded. 'Codeine usually does the trick in no time flat. Dr. McTavish is right. You have concussion; two days in bed for you, my lad.'

Tim lay back on the pillow. Two days in bed! It would be like being back in the sick room at boarding school a few weeks ago; he'd hated that.

'You had us so worried, son. Mum was certain you'd swallowed some of that filthy water.'

Tim felt his stomach heave. That would have been awful! He stared up at his father. Major Athelstan was in uniform: khaki battle-dress trousers and a light-cotton khaki shirt with a plain khaki tie. A thin white streak of hair, running from front to back through the middle of his fair, sandy hair was emphasized by the early morning sunlight streaming in through the bedroom window.

Two years ago in 1945, when Dad had returned to England, Tim hadn't been able to stop staring. He hadn't recognized Dad. He wasn't like the handsome soldier in the photo that he and Sarah would sneak in to see on Mum's dresser in her bedroom. It wasn't just the streak of white hair or the slight limp; Dad had changed! He was extremely thin, and his movements had been slow like an old man. And he wasn't the fun Dad that Tim had remembered and had waited for.

Now, two years later, apart from his hair and his hands, Dad seemed to be returning to his old self. Tim seldom noticed the streak of white anymore but he couldn't ignore Dad's hands; they never seemed to be still, the fingers of one hand alternately rubbing the fingertips of the other. There were no nails, only shiny skin where the nails had once been. Tim shivered as he thought of the torture Dad had endured at the hands of the Nazi SS officer. The SS officer was in prison and would soon be tried in a war-crimes court in Hamburg. Dad was a prime witness.

'You are absolutely positive you didn't swallow any, Tim?'

'No, Dad. I got some on me but it was on my body, on my back, not on my head. I didn't swallow any, I know I didn't.'

'Good! But we'll keep an eye on you just the same; can't be too careful with all this sickness going around.'

Tim knew what his father meant. Almost the first things Mum had shown him on arriving at the house were the large stainless steel jugs kept in the refrigerator. That was another thing, the refrigerator; Tim had never seen one in a house before.

'I boil water every day on the stove in the basement,' said Mum. 'There are jugs in the refrigerator down there too. Only drink boiled water, Tim; the Hamburg area water system was so badly damaged by the bombing that some parts are still contaminated by sewage. Many people have been sick with dysentery; and many have died from Cholera and Typhoid because they drank bad water.'

Tim shivered. No, he hadn't swallowed any of that filthy water.

'Was it a bomb, Dad, a UXB?' Tim looked up.

'Was what a bomb, son?'

'Yesterday, Dad. The explosion.'

'No, son.' Dad smiled. 'Hamburg was badly hit by Allied bombing, especially near the docks. You saw that when you arrived last week. But I don't believe any bombs, even strays, reached this area. Of course, down by the river there may still be unexploded bombs in the ruins, but we've no reports of UXBs around here in Alstemarschen.'

Tim nodded then wished he hadn't. His head hurt and his brain seemed to bounce around inside. 'Then what was it, Dad?'

'It was the main sewer that runs beneath Schulhaus Strasse, Tim. It was a massive explosion; it had to be to force the sewage up through the pipes like that.'

Tim could smell the stench all over again.

Dad continued: 'There's an enormous hole in the road, down that way.' He pointed across the room, out of the window. 'It's round the corner, opposite the cemetery, near Welch's house. It's like a bomb crater. Many of the gravestones were shattered or flattened.' Dad shook his head. 'The smell is atrocious!'

'From the graves, Dad?'

Major Athelstan laughed. 'No son. There are no open graves, although quite a few tombstones were toppled. The smell is from the open sewer.'

'Oh!' Tim breathed in carefully. That's what he could smell. It wasn't his imagination. But there was another strong smell mixed with it, a pungent smell. Disinfectant! Now he remembered. Mum had told him she had Inge scrub out the bathroom with Dettol. 'How did the sewer blow up, Dad?'

'Gas, Tim. Sewer gas is highly explosive. But I'm not sure what set it off. The police are investigating, the local German police and our military police. I was called down to have a look, but as I said, it wasn't a bomb. There's a suggestion it has something to do with the black market.'

Tim remembered the crowds of people outside Hamburg railway station last week. Dad had met him at Cuxhaven when he got off the ship and they had travelled to Hamburg together. Dad had pointed at the crowds. 'See all those people, Tim?'

'Yes, Dad.' There were hundreds of people hanging around the station out in the open. 'Where are they going?'

'They aren't going anywhere. They're trading on the black market.' Dad nodded. 'It's illegal. But even though it is two years since the war ended, the food situation here in Germany is so bad that many people barter for food, much of it stolen, if they want to eat.'

Tim remembered hearing on the BBC news a report about a massive demonstration in Hamburg, a food strike by over a hundred thousand union workers. They complained that they couldn't work because they were so hungry.

Dad also pointed out the crowds on the Reeperbahn as they drove out of Hamburg on the way home, and another large crowd at the Altona station.

'See those boys, Tim?'

A lot of boys were dodging in and out of the crowd.

'Many of them are about twelve or thirteen years old, about your age.'

Tim looked closer. The boys were very thin and poorly dressed.

'They are most likely exchanging coffee or cigarettes for food. Cigarettes can be traded for fifty times what they're actually worth.'

'But how do they get the cigarettes, Dad?'

'They've probably traded with the troops, traded things they've stolen; or perhaps even family valuables: jewels, costly furs, cameras, silver and china and things like that.'

That was the black market.

But now, thinking of the present Tim was confused. 'What have the sewers got to do with the black market, Dad?'

Dad rubbed the tips of his fingers together. 'There are criminal gangs known to use the sewers as a hidden transportation system, Tim; others use the sewers as a way to escape the police.'

'Are the sewers that big, Dad?'

'Oh, yes, the main ones are. They're eight, maybe ten feet wide; they make a perfect underground road system if you don't mind the smell and the rats. It's a secret network for anyone up to no good, anyone who doesn't want to be caught.'

'Then why blow it up, Dad?'

'Ah.' Dad nodded. 'I don't think it was blown up on purpose, Tim. Remember I said that sewer gas was very dangerous? Well, I would think it was an accident; some fool lighting a cigarette; something like that would ignite the gas. If so, and if the police are lucky, they may find the bodies in the rubble.' He shook his head. 'But I doubt it. Terrible explosion!'

Tim shivered. He felt cold beneath the bedclothes. The explosion, talk of gas and of people being buried, brought memories flooding back of a terrible night in 1940 when their house in England had been bombed; memories of the gas mask and being buried in the wreckage of the air raid shelter in the garden of their home in London. He hadn't thought of that for a long time.

'What's the matter, son?' Dad sat on the edge of the bed.

Tim breathed in deeply and brought his focus back to the present. It was seven years since that terrible night.

He'd been five at the time. It was now May of 1947. The war had been over for two years. There were no more bombs falling, no more hated gas masks, he knew that. And he was in the British zone of Germany, safe with Dad and the rest of the family. But thinking of that night still gave him the shivers.

'Nothing, Dad,' he said. 'Nothing really, but the explosion made me think of our old house in England, at Hampstead. When the bomb hit they had to dig me out of the shelter. And I was thinking of poor old Bits.'

Dad's lips formed a thin hard line beneath his bristling, close-clipped fair moustache. Bits had been Dad's dog, an old mongrel with little bits of all the dog breeds in him, or so Dad used to say. Bits had died the night the bomb hit. Dad sighed and nodded slowly.

'Poor old Bits,' he said. 'After all these years I still miss that old dog.'

'So do I, Dad.' Tim looked up into his father's dark brown eyes. They were sad. He tried to change the subject. 'Mum said you'd tell me about Mr. Welch, Dad. It was Reggie Welch who challenged me to that race.'

Dad nodded. 'I will, but I don't have time this morning, son; Heinz is waiting to drive me into headquarters in Hamburg. But I will tell you.' He stood up.

Dad reached out with his right hand and gently stroked Tim's forehead. The smooth, nail-less ends of the fingers felt funny, but soothing.

'I'll tell Mum you're ready for breakfast, Tim. Scrambled eggs, powdered eggs of course, with tinned Danish bacon and fried bread. Eat up, then try to rest.'

Chapter 3

MINES AND MASHED POTATOES

Tim felt comfortably full. Breakfast had been super. The tinned bacon was really good and he loved powdered scrambled eggs. When they had eggs during the war they were usually powdered eggs as the ration for fresh eggs was only one a month. One thing though, he hoped they wouldn't have to drink tinned milk in tea all the time.

He snuggled down in bed. It was strange, not like his bed in England or at boarding school; there were no blankets or sheets, just two very large eiderdowns, one on the bottom and one on top. And they weren't really eiderdowns. Tim tried to remember what Mum had called them. They were filled with soft feathers like an eiderdown, only much thicker. Ah yes, that's right, they were called a 'federbett'. Sarah said you hung them out of the window on fine days to air them and make them fresh. It was odd really, but at least making the bed would be easy, not like at boarding school where the sheets and blankets had to be perfectly smooth, with 'boxed' corners folded neatly like brown paper at the corner of a parcel. And it certainly wouldn't be as difficult as making up his bunk on the ship that had brought him from England to Germany.

Tim had enjoyed the two days on the Empire Halladale, crossing the North Sea from Tilbury in England to Cuxhaven in Germany. There were two other boys in his cabin but they hadn't been any fun and he didn't get to know them as they were seasick all the time.

Grandma Rose and Grandpa George saw him onto the train at St. Pancras railway station in London. Grandma made sure he had the small, shiny enamel British Union Jack flag pinned firmly onto the lapel of his jacket. It was his blue flannel school jacket, but Grandma had taken the old school badge off the pocket. 'You're never going back to a school like that where they half-starve you,' she said. And Grandpa had agreed.

At St. Pancras station they'd met a Dutch girl who was to look after him and the two other boys on the voyage to Germany. She was nice. She was married to a Canadian soldier she'd met when the Netherlands were liberated. She'd been a member of the Dutch Resistance and had almost been caught by the Gestapo on two occasions as she was sending messages to England on a hidden underground radio transmitter. The girl's story reminded Tim of his own radio, the crystal set he'd made during the war. He'd picked up a few messages on the crystal set, messages sent by the Resistance, although at first he didn't know what they were, or that they were secret coded messages.

Whenever he thought of the crystal set he could hear the strange heavily accented foreign voice that had sung the old English folk song, Widdecombe Fair. And whenever Widdecombe Fair had crackled through the earphones of the crystal radio it was always the same man's voice. The song was a secret code the Resistance man used to send the names of missing soldiers and airmen across the airwaves to England; this told the Army and Air Force that the men were safe and hidden from the Nazis.

At the time Tim knew nothing of the secret code, but then, just before Christmas 1944, he'd heard the Resistance man sing Dad's name, and the name of Dad's sergeant in the song. He couldn't believe it at first, but he'd heard it again. Tim sighed. At first Mum hadn't believed him either when he told her Dad was safe. But a few days later, just before Christmas, a telegram arrived from the War Office, delivered by a soldier on a khaki-coloured motorcycle. Dad was safe and in hiding. And although Widdecombe Fair wasn't a Christmas song, whenever Tim heard it now he always thought of Christmas and that special Christmas in 1944.

Tim finished his tea. It was cold and tasted tinny and metallic, but he was thirsty. He wished Mum would come upstairs but she was getting Sarah ready for school.

Tim lay back thinking of the journey on The Empire Halladale, across the North Sea from England to Germany. The sea had been really rough and many people were seasick. But he hadn't been sick. Grandpa had spent his early life at sea and had told him he must eat if he didn't want to be violently sick. Grandpa said that eating would make him feel good, whatever the sea conditions were like. It had worked. And the food had been super, not like at boarding school, where dinner every night except Sunday and Wednesday had been baked beans and potatoes in their jackets, the skin on the potatoes as tough as leather from being baked in the oven too long. Dinner on Wednesday was tripe and onions, white and sloppy in thin runny gravy. Why would anyone want to eat cow's stomach? And the tripe was always followed by Tapioca pudding which everyone called frog's eyes. His teeth ached as he remembered. He'd thought the food at school had been bad because food was still rationed, even two years after the war. But on the head table, where the housemaster and the seniors and prefects had their meals, there was always meat and vegetables with a choice of cheese and fruit afterwards. And it always smelled so good!

When Tim became sick he lay for days in the boarding school sick room covered in boils, tossing and turning at night, until one day Grandpa had come to the school. Grandpa was furious when he discovered that Tim's ration of cheese, butter and meat had been used for the head table.

'No wonder the boy is sick!' he had shouted.

Grandpa didn't often get angry but he'd confronted the headmaster and taken Tim out of the school there and then, insisting that Tim join the rest of the family in Germany.

The voyage on the ship had been exciting. The captain had to steer through narrow channels marked by buoys to avoid mines, deadly explosives that often lurked just beneath the surface. Tim stood at the rail, watching the creamy-white wake of the ship as it ploughed its way through the sea, imagining he was the captain of a battleship or a destroyer, searching the seas for mines and

U-boats. There were no more submarines, no U-Boats of course, but even now there was real danger from mines that as yet hadn't been cleared from the sea.

He wondered what Mum would make for lunch. The food onboard ship had been incredible. He remembered lunch on the first day: there was thick vegetable soup, grilled cod with carrots, onions, mashed turnips, mashed potatoes, tinned peas and butter sauce; and then a steamed jam pudding with stewed apples and custard. It was incredible!

Tim sighed and snuggled deeper into the pillow pulling the feather-filled cover up beneath his chin. He wondered what it would be like now that he was here in Germany. Had the war changed Dad so much? The trial of the SS officer was coming up soon, in a month or two. Just yesterday Mum had said:

'It will be a terrible time for Dad.' Mum shook her head. 'He will have to recall the torture he went through. So don't ask Dad about it, Tim. And don't worry if Dad is distant or angry at times.'

But Dad had seemed pleased to see him when he'd picked him up at Cuxhaven. And yesterday, after the explosion, he'd been very concerned.

And what was it about Mr. Welch that made Dad dislike him? And then there was Reggie; Tim knew Reggie would be a problem.

Chapter 4

A THIEF?

It was early Friday morning, the first day Captain McTavish allowed Tim out of bed. Last night Mum said there was no point in him going back to the British Families Education Service School until Tuesday, the day after the Whit Monday holiday; by then he should be fully recovered. That suited Tim just fine, as he wanted to explore the house.

He slipped out of bed. His black tin trunk was beneath the window where Heinz, Dad's driver, had placed it three days ago. It was an army officers' campaign trunk, an old one that Dad repainted when Tim went to boarding school. Grandpa had blacked out the school address and, in large white letters had painted the new address in Germany.

T.A.ATHELSTAN ESQ.
7, GUSTAV STRASSE,
ALSTEMARSCHEN, HAMBURG, GERMANY
B.A.O.R.

Tim stood on the lid of the trunk and looked out of the half-open window. Number seven Gustav Strasse, or Gustav Strasse sieben, as Sarah had corrected him last night, was a large red brick house situated on a curve in the street. When Sarah said 'sieben' she made a whistling sound; her two top middle teeth were missing. Sarah knew quite a lot of German and chatted away with Inge. So did 'baby' Jane.

Because the house was on a bend in the road it had a very large garden, wide at the back and narrow in the front, a wedge like a large piece of pie. The back garden was separated from fields beyond by a thick hedge. Mum said the hedge was beechnut. The first field was a potato field; cabbages and turnips grew in the fields beyond. The potato plants were a deep green colour and reminded him of the backfield at Medbury where he'd lived during the war and where he'd played parachutes with his old friend, Bob. He wondered if Bob still had that Luftwaffe flare parachute.

Tim was attracted by movement in the near, right corner of the field. There was someone there, bent over. Tim leaned out of the window to see more clearly. As if sensing this, the person turned and looked up at him. It was a boy with very short dark hair, raggedly dressed. He darted furtively to the right, running, clutching something close to his chest. Then he disappeared behind the house next door.

There was something familiar about the boy. Maybe he was one of the boy's Tim had seen at the station in Hamburg or at the black market on the Reeperbahn or at Altona? He shook his head. No, that wasn't it. Then he remembered. There was a boy outside the house when he'd arrived with Dad. That was it! The boy had close-cropped dark hair and his clothes, old and tattered hung on him like rags. And he wore funny sandals. He'd put his tongue out at Tim. But it was the way he ran that Tim remembered now, as if the odd-looking sandals were going to fly off. Dad hadn't seen the boy; he'd been too busy talking to Heinz, who'd met them at Hamburg station in a khaki-painted Volkswagen.

'He's new round here,' Mum had said at tea that first day. 'From the way you describe him, Tim I know I haven't seen him before. I expect we'll have him begging at the door any day now.'

'Well make sure it's not more than begging,' said Dad. 'Some of those children are master thieves, especially those with no homes, no parents. They steal to live. They break into houses and steal food, or steal items they can exchange for food on the blackmarket. Remember me pointing them out as we passed the station at Altona, Tim?'

Tim nodded. He wondered if the boy was a thief.

'Poor little mites,' said Mum. She seemed to hesitate then smiled as she handed round the plate of sandwiches. 'Eat up, everyone! I don't want to see any of these left. I was lucky to find this shrimp paste at the NAAFI shop.'

Dad took a sandwich. 'Mm! They're very good.'

Tim watched his father chewing, his bristly fair moustache moving rhythmically up and down. Tim wanted more to eat but this talk of children begging and stealing to eat made him feel awkward, and made him think of boarding school when he was always hungry. Sarah leaned forward and took another sandwich.

'Mm! I love these sandwiches, Mum.' Sarah smiled and took a bite.

It was too much for Tim. He put two sandwiches on his plate. As he was about to bite into the first Dad said:

'Talking of mites, Tim, you steer clear of that boy if he's around. It sounds as if he's had his head shaved. He probably has lice.'

Tim's eyes widened. Lice! They carried disease! Typhus! First there was bad water, and now lice!

'Well, Tim wouldn't associate with him,' said Mum. 'Why would he?' She shrugged. 'I know they've stopped that non-fraternizing rule, but there are plenty of British children round here.'

'What's non fraternizing?' said Tim.

'Fraternizing? It means being friendly with the enemy, son.' Dad looked grim. 'We don't do that.' Slowly he rubbed the tips of his fingers together.

Now, as he stood at his bedroom window, Tim recalled that tea almost a week ago. The shrimp paste had been super. He hadn't had shrimp paste for ages. But best of all were the cucumber sandwiches. Dad had picked an early cucumber from the greenhouse. If only there could have been some Tate and Lyle golden syrup. Mm! Treacle syrup sandwiches were incredible! And treacle tart was even better!

Inge, Mum's German maid, had waited in the background while they ate, to pour more tea. Tim wanted to ask more about fraternizing, about being friendly with the enemy. Dad was friendly with Heinz. Could he be friends with Heinz, and with Inge? And what about the man who tended the boilers in the basement and who was also the gardener? But he thought he'd better not ask, and anyway he was embarrassed in front of Inge. Then, when Inge took 'baby' Jane to get her ready for bed and he heard all the giggling and laughing he was really confused. Was that fraternizing? He didn't want to ask. Dad had been so stern when he'd talked about it. Being friendly with the enemy? You didn't do that!

Tim breathed in deeply. The fields looked so peaceful. The house was quiet. It must be very early. He breathed in again but not so deeply this time. The only thing that spoiled the beauty of the morning was the lingering smell from the sewer. It must be awful down at the Welch's house. He nodded. The police still hadn't found out who had been in the sewer, or if the explosion was connected to the black market. It was interesting. Maybe he'd ask Mum if he could go and look at the crater; Sarah said it was enormous; she passed it every day on the way to school. At first there had been concern that the water supply in Alstemarschen could be damaged, but only one supply line had ruptured and it was quickly repaired. The sewer would take much longer.

Tim moved slowly back to bed, careful not to make any noise. He picked up the silver pocket watch Grandpa George had given him. It was only five to six. Boy! It really was early. Inge wouldn't bring tea until seven. He climbed into bed, snuggled back into the pillow and closed his eyes. What had that boy been doing? What was he hiding? Had he stolen something, was he a thief?

Gradually he became aware that it had started to rain. Maybe the rain would wash away the sewer smell. The steady rhythmic patter of raindrops was so soothing that Tim drifted back off to sleep.

Chapter 5

GUSTAV STRASSE SIEBEN

Tim wanted to explore the house before the girls came home. Jane was at a friend's house. Sarah was at a small school in a private house in the village. The teacher was Mrs. Beecher the wife of an army officer; she ran the school. Tim's school was in Altona, two miles away.

'Mrs. Beecher was a teacher before the war, Tim. She started the school when she arrived here last September.' Mum pushed a lock of wavy light brown hair from her forehead. She had grown her hair quite long since she'd been in Germany. Dad said he liked it that way. 'The Beechers live on our side of the road, Tim, four houses down.' Mum locked the pantry door and hung a large bunch of keys on her belt. 'She doesn't have children of her own and it gives her something to do while Captain Beecher is at work. She's a good teacher. Sarah's doing well.'

Tim was barely aware of what Mum was saying. He stared at the keys dangling from Mum's belt. Why did Mum always lock everything up? She locked the pantry, the larder, and the cupboard where the pots and pans were hung.

'What's the matter, Tim?'

'Those keys, Mum. Why do you lock everything?'

Mum shook her head. Her blue eyes narrowed as she frowned. 'Before Inge we had a maid called Hilda. I noticed the food rations didn't last very long; the tea went quickly, butter, bread, everything.'

'Was she stealing, Mum?'

'Yes, Tim. We caught her at it. It wasn't just food, though. Dad kept cutting his face when he shaved. Hilda was putting used razor blades in Dad's new packets and taking out the new ones and selling them.'

'On the black market, Mum?'

Mum shrugged. 'I suppose so. I hadn't really thought about it. But it made me really mad! It wasn't just Dad cutting himself with blunt blades, but Hilda ate with us and shared our food. That meant her parents had her ration book as well as their own. Dad told her to leave immediately. We didn't find Inge until two weeks later. Meanwhile I'd spoken to other wives who'd had the same trouble. They had locks fitted. I did too.' Mum shrugged. 'Now I lock everything.'

Tim thought about this. He didn't really know Inge but she seemed very nice. Jane loved her. Inge was twenty-four and Mum said she was an excellent cook with very little to work with. Mum should know, the way she'd made tasty meals out of almost nothing during the war.

'Inge makes a delicious meal with potatoes and apples called Himmel und Erde.'

'Potatoes and apples?' Tim couldn't imagine that. 'What does it mean, Mum, himmel und erde?'

'Heaven and earth, Tim: Apples from on high and potatoes from the earth. I'll get Inge to make it for you sometime. The girls love it. Dad and I like it too.'

Tim nodded. Maybe it would taste good. It would be interesting to see what else Inge would cook. Inge was slightly shorter than Mum, only about five feet four inches; and she was quite plump. She had very curly dark brown hair, almost black, and when she smiled there were dimples in her cheeks. Her eyes attracted Tim; they were a green colour and full of fun.

'Do you think Inge would steal, Mum?'

'No.' Mum shook her head, the lock of light brown hair falling down over her forehead again. 'I don't think so. But if the temptation isn't there I don't have to worry, do I?' She smiled, pushing the hair away from her eyes. 'Anyway, my lad, time to boil the water for today.' She took the two stainless steel jugs from the kitchen counter. 'I'll be in the basement for a while. Do you want to come?'

Tim shook his head. He'd seen the basement the day he'd arrived and when he'd stripped off his clothes after Reggie Welch had tricked him. It was huge with an unfinished concrete floor and thick concrete walls about ten feet high. It was warm down there and smelled of coal. There was a mountain of shiny black nuggets that fed the enormous black, cast iron boiler. Tim had been amazed. The boiler heated the whole house! In England they'd huddled round the fire in the living room and taken hot water bottles to bed.

The place that interested Tim most in the basement was the large bomb shelter. The ceiling was reinforced with steel railway track. More rails were embedded in the walls. Iron tubes led down from above to provide fresh air. There were two thick steel doors hung on massive hinges; they reminded Tim of ships doors on the Empire Halladale; each one opened with a large brass lever. One door led into the shelter from the basement, the other out to the garden. This shelter wouldn't have collapsed like the Anderson shelter in the garden collapsed when their London house was bombed and Tim had been buried.

'Where does the owner of this house live?' Tim had asked.

'On a boat, Tim, somewhere on the Elbe. He's one of the lucky ones.'

'Why doesn't he live here?'

Mum nodded slowly. 'Well, Tim, you must understand that when people lose a war things are difficult. For us to be here with Dad we need a house. So do other families. Houses are requisitioned, taken from the owners for the time we're here. All the houses in this area, all the way to the Country Club, have been requisitioned, except for the farmhouse and the house in the orchard. But as I said, the man who owns this house is lucky; he had somewhere to go, one of his boats. He owns a shipping line or something like that. Other people aren't so lucky; they must move in with relatives or friends, or even with strangers. I've heard of three or four families sharing a house. Some families even share a room.'

Tim tried to imagine three or four families crammed into the cottage at Medbury. Suppose Hitler had invaded and conquered England and the Nazis had taken Bramley Cottage? Suppose they'd also taken Grandpa's House at

Corveston? Where would the family have lived? It would have been terrible! He shivered.

'Are you cold, Tim?'

'No, Mum. I was just imagining what it would have been like if Hitler had won the war and conquered England.'

'It doesn't bear thinking about.' Mum pointed to the door at the far end of the shelter. 'That door leads to the garden but we can't open it. The padlock has a combination but we don't know the number. Dad said he'd cut the lock off and put another one on. But there's no point. We won't use it.'

The only other place of interest in the basement was the garage. A concrete driveway sloped steeply down from above, shut off by two heavy wooden doors.

'This is where Dad keeps his private car, Tim, an Opal. During the week Heinz drives Dad in the Volkswagen.' Mum smiled. 'But on weekends Dad likes to drive his own car.'

Tim hadn't seen an Opal before. He thought it was super. It was highly polished, with deep dark green paint and a shiny chrome trim. The dashboard was polished wood, the seats a dark brown leather.

'Some of the neighbours, like Mr. Welch, laugh when we go out in this car.'

Tim couldn't believe this. It was a really wizard car a bit like Grandpa's. 'Why would they laugh, Mum?'

'It's an old car, Tim, pre-war. Many of the neighbours have new cars, mostly Mercedes. But this one is so comfortable; you sink right into the seats. It's like being in a coach.'

Tim nodded slowly. Today was Friday. Tomorrow they'd be going in the Opal to shop at the NAAFI. But right now Tim wanted to explore the attic. He hadn't been up there yet and it sounded interesting. He wanted to explore before Sarah came home; she didn't have school after lunch on Fridays.

'Can I explore the attic, Mum?'

'If you want to, Tim. Just one thing, though!' Mum's blue eyes took on a serious look. 'The room on the left, at the top of the stairs, is Inge's. Don't go in there, please. The other two rooms are full of oddments, old furniture, things like that, nothing of interest.'

The stairs were steep; a narrow blue and red carpet runner fastened with brass rails made them seem even more steep; seven steps up to a small landing, then six more to another larger landing and four white-painted doors. The one to the immediate left was shut; that must be Inge's. The door straight ahead was open and Tim could see old chairs, stools and boxes piled higgledy-piggledy. He opened the door immediately to his right. It too contained dusty old furniture, but not a lot, and it wasn't topsy-turvy. Tim opened the fourth door, a bathroom, Inge's. Mum had forgotten to tell him that. He closed the door and entered the room to his right.

There was dust everywhere. Three sets of side-by-side windows looked out over the back garden. The windows were dirty; raindrops slithered slowly down, struggling against the clinging pull of the greenish grime on the glass. There was a small dust-covered desk with a chair, two glass-fronted bookcases crammed with hard-backed books, many with gold lettering on the spine, and two upholstered chairs each with a footstool in the same maroon velvet material. Paintings and photographs crowded the walls; they were mostly of ships. But what caught Tim's eye was a tripod near the window. Mounted on the tripod were binoculars, the biggest Tim had ever seen. They were more than a foot long, probably about eighteen inches, painted a dull light grey.

Tim couldn't look through the binoculars, the tripod was too high. He pulled over one of the footstools. It was soft and he wobbled before getting his balance. Then he held onto the binoculars and looked through the eyepieces. It was as if they had been adjusted and set up just for him. Through the grimy windows he looked over the fields through the trees to a river. It must be the Elbe. He moved his head to one side to orient himself. The binoculars pointed through the windows on the right. It couldn't be those trees he was seeing, could it? They seemed miles away! He peered through the binoculars again. Yes, it was those trees! Without the binoculars he could barely see the river. This was incredible!

He swung the glasses to the left. There were ruins by the river, to the left more ruins. A small figure clambered awkwardly over a pile of rubble then disappeared as if swallowed by broken bricks. All was still.

'Tim! Tim! Elevenses! Tea time!'

Chapter 6

THE CAMERA

'Come on!' said Dad after breakfast on Saturday morning. 'Everyone into the car! We're off to Hamburg to shop at the NAAFI.'

Tim settled into the back seat of the Opal. It really was very comfortable. Even on bad roads pock-marked with potholes the bumps were barely noticeable. As the car purred along past Altona, along König Strasse and the Reeperbahn Tim couldn't help but notice the terrible destruction. Cobbled side roads, although cleared of rubble, were more like narrow lanes through a rocky wilderness. And most of the streets were unmarked; if street signs remained they were so bent and twisted that he couldn't read the names.

The pile-upon-pile of fire-blackened rubble was depressing. In some places weeds and flowers grew in cracks between the broken bricks. In the distance, to his left, the spire of a church pointed, untouched, skyward out of the ruins. Then to his right he saw clothes hanging out to dry on a makeshift clothesline strung between a crumbling brick chimney and a twisted metal girder.

'Hey! Look at that!' he said.

'People live there,' said Sarah. 'They probably live in a basement. Lots of people live in basements in the ruins.'

Mum nodded. 'That's right. Remember what I told you, Tim? Finding anywhere to live is so difficult, especially for the refugees from eastern Germany. They're glad to have anywhere to call home.' She shook her head. 'What some of those places must have been like during last winter I can't imagine? It was bitterly cold.'

'A fight for survival,' said Dad. 'And don't forget the orphans.'

'Orphans, Dad?'

'Yes, Tim. At one time there were over three thousand living like animals in holes in the ground. There are still children living in the ruins, gangs of young thieves, stealing and trading on the black market.'

'Like Oliver Twist and the Artful Dodger,' said Tim.

'Yes. I suppose you could say that. Anyway, do you see any wood in the ruins, Tim?'

Tim looked out of the car window. The talk of orphans had given the ruins a new fascination and he remembered the small figure he'd seen through the binoculars. Was that one of the orphans? But he was puzzled. What did Dad mean about wood? There were no trees; he'd noticed that earlier. Now he saw there were no doors, no frames, and window openings in walls still standing were bare to the bricks and concrete blocks.

'I can't see any wood, Dad. There isn't any, not even door or window frames.'

'Right, son. Every scrap of wood has been scavenged for fires and stoves. What will happen this coming winter, if conditions don't improve, I don't know. And I don't care to think about it.'

Dad changed gear, slowing down as they approached an intersection.

'Careful!' shouted Mum.

An old woman, head down and shoulders hunched, was halfway across the road. The car came to a shuddering halt, tires screeching on the cobblestones.

'Phew! That was close, Dad.'

The old woman turned her head sharply and looked at the car in surprise. There was fear in her eyes as she pulled her knitted woolen coat tightly about her scrawny body and ran, limping to the far side of the road.

'Poor old dear,' said Mum. 'She's lucky Dad was driving. No one stops or even slows down for pedestrians here; if anything they seem to speed up. Just you remember that, Tim.'

'I will, Mum.'

As the car picked up speed Tim stared out at the passing ruins. Many of the walls that remained standing had words painted on them, stark white letters on the cracked and crumbling bricks: WEG MIT HITLER! WEG MIT KRIEG!

'What are those words on the walls, Mum?'

'Messages, Tim. People paint messages on the walls telling family and friends where they've gone.'

'But what's that about Hitler?' he asked.

'Oh! I know that,' said Sarah. 'You mean the one that says DOWN WITH HITLER. DOWN WITH WAR.'

'Well, what about that one?' said Tim, pointing. 'The one that says DER FUHRER KANN MIR…'

Dad cleared his throat noisily. 'Some of the messages are a bit rude, Tim. That's another one about Hitler, but you don't need to know what it says.'

'Him!' Tim looked at Sarah but she shook her head. She silently mouthed the words: 'I don't know,' and continued shaking her head.

'Now there's an interesting one.' Mum pointed across the road. 'I haven't seen that one before.'

'Where, Mum?' Sarah was peering out of the window.

'There! See it? It says 'Alstermarschen'.'

Alstemarschen! That's where they lived! Tim looked at the crumbling brick wall. ERICA – ALSTEMARSCHEN. It wasn't well painted but the letters were big and easy to read.

Mum was continuing. 'Probably someone telling their family they've gone to Alstemarschen.'

'That's right,' said Dad. 'Heinz told me the other day that some of the messages are new. Families have lost touch with men who were prisoners of war and who are now returning. They leave messages hoping that when the men return to what used to be home they'll see the message and know where to find them, or start looking.'

'It's like when we were bombed out the second time, Dad,' said Tim. 'I knew you wouldn't know where we were, that we'd moved to Medbury. Then we heard you were missing in action.'

'Right,' said Dad, quietly.

Mum turned and looked at Tim, frowning. She shook her head slowly and raised a finger to her lips.

The NAAFI, the British Families Shop run by the Navy, Army and Air Force Institute was in the centre of Hamburg in Grosse Bleichen. It had once been a hotel. You couldn't see in from the outside because the lower windows were shuttered in concrete to keep envious eyes from peering in. Mum said there were all sorts of things in the shop she hadn't seen since before the war. There were special biscuits, all kinds of sauces and her favorite salad dressing. But Tim wasn't interested in walking around looking at food so he stayed in the entrance hall where there were wooden cabinets with glass doors filled with all kinds of interesting things.

In one of the cabinets, high on a shelf was a box camera. The lady who sat behind the old hotel reception desk, half-hidden behind ferns in a huge pot, smiled at him and got up from her tubular steel chair.

'You like?' she said. 'I show you.' She took a key from a drawer in the desk and came over to the cabinet. 'It is camera you look at, ja?'

Tim nodded as the woman unlocked the cabinet and reached up. She took out the camera and gave it to Tim. 'You look,' she said.

Tim held the camera. It was black and had several shiny, silver levers and two viewing lenses. He held the camera at waist height and looked down through one of the rectangular lenses. The lens shone with rainbow colours, but he could see the reception desk clearly. Above the lens, in shiny letters, was the word BILORA. There was a short leather handle on top. Tim looked at the price written on a ticket attached to the handle. The camera wasn't too expensive. He calculated that with the pocket money Dad said he'd give him every Saturday he could buy the camera by the end of summer. He'd wanted a camera for a long time. Slowly, he handed the camera back to the lady.

'Thank you,' he said. 'Danke.'

The lady nodded and smiled. 'Bitte schoen.' She put the camera back on the shelf and locked the door.

Tim nodded absently. He was thinking. This morning, when Dad had given him the pocket money, he didn't know what it was. It was brown bakalite and was called Baffs. Tim knew the coins were bakalite because he'd seen the plastic-like material before. Dad explained that the name stood for British Armed Forces Vouchers: it was the only money you could use in the NAAFI, to prevent trading on the black market. Tim didn't quite understand that but he set his mind on saving for the box camera.

The camera would be fun.

He told Dad about it later and Dad said he'd find out if he could get the materials to set up a darkroom for developing; they could use the shelter in the basement.

Chapter 7

THUMP! THUMP! THUMP!

Tuesday came quickly.

At dinner on Monday evening Dad said: 'Avoid young Welch, Tim. He's obviously like his father and that means he's trouble.'

Tim knew Reggie Welch was trouble. He'd avoid him if he could, but Welch sat behind him in class.

Dad shook his head. 'I never could get on with Welch. He was a slimy little creep when he was a corporal and worse when he made sergeant. He's the type who makes trouble without drawing attention to himself and then profits from the problem by seeming to know how to solve it. That's how he got that battlefield commission.' Dad pursed his lips, his fair moustache bristling

Dad rubbed the ends of his fingers and Tim saw his hands trembling.

'What happened, Dad?'

Dad breathed in deeply, staring out of the dining room window. 'I won't go into details, but Welch was in a party building a Bailey bridge across a river. Problems developed and the enemy concentrated artillery fire on the crossing. The young officer in charge was killed but not before they had the bridge all but in place. The German artillery was knocked out by our aircraft and Welch took over. He made a report in his own favour. The battalion commander thought Welch was responsible for the success of the bridge-building operation and promoted him to officer rank.'

'But didn't Mr. Welch say that the officer who was killed was really responsible, Dad?'

Dad laughed, a short, sharp, hollow sound. He shook his head. 'Not our Mr. Welch, Tim. He took the credit, our troops were advancing and in the heat of battle the days passed quickly and the incident was soon forgotten; but not by me. I've never forgotten it.'

'Then, when the war was over and Welch was demobbed out of the army, I thought that was the last I'd see of him. Huh!' Dad shook his head. 'The only reason the little toad got out of the army and back into civvies was to wangle his way into the CCG and come back to Germany. Now he's the same equivalent as me.'

'What do you mean, equivalent, Dad?'

'Well he's no longer commissioned, no longer an officer, Tim, but in the CCG they have a ranking system depending on what they do. He has a rank equivalent to that of a major in the army. He is, supposedly an expert in Supplies Distribution.' Dad shook his head slowly. 'Supplies Distribution! Huh! I often wonder what gets distributed and where to.'

'Well, from what I hear, we may not have to put up with the Welch family being near us much longer,' said Mum. 'I was speaking to Muriel Welch only this morning.'

'You were talking to Welch's wife?' Dad's voice was raised in surprise. 'Welch's wife?'

'Yes I was,' said Mum. Her blue eyes flashed as she pushed a lock of brown hair away from her forehead. 'The poor woman! She's really quite nice. From what I hear Cyril Welch gives her a really hard time. Anyway, she's asked him to get them moved from Pooh Corner.'

'Pooh Corner.' Dad chuckled. 'I like that name.' He laughed again. 'Can't say I blame Mrs. Welch; having a house next to an open sewer must be terrible, especially on a hot sunny day.' Dad shook his head. 'Anyway, son,' he turned to Tim. 'Avoid young Welch. That's an order.'

But Tim couldn't avoid Reggie Welch. In class, behind him, Welch sat kicking at the legs of Tim's chair. Thump! Thump! Thump! When Tim turned round to ask him to stop, Welch just grinned. It went on.

'Athelstan!' How many times do I have to tell you to face the front? Get on with your work!' The class teacher peered at Tim through thick-lensed glasses. 'And stop bothering Welch.'

Tim ground his teeth as he heard Welch chuckle quietly. This wasn't a good start. From the time he'd entered the classroom last week, Mr. Morgan had seemed to be annoyed with him. Why? It wasn't his fault he'd had to join the class midway through the term. And anyway it was Welch's fault that he'd been sent home on the first day and had been in the bath when the explosion occurred. He still had occasional headaches. And then

Welch was constantly kicking his chair. Looking up he saw the teacher staring at him.

Mr. Morgan was a short, thin man. His straggly dark brown hair was combed over to the right side of his head from low on the left side just above his ear; the hair only partially covered a large bald spot.

'And, Athelstan, don't ask again about changing places. We had no complaints with the seating arrangements until you arrived.'

Thump! Tim felt his chair being kicked again. He heard Welch snigger. He gritted his teeth. He didn't want any more trouble with Welch, not after what Dad had said. But he knew Mr. Morgan wouldn't give him a good report. Why did he have to join the school at the end of the month when report cards were issued?

'Try not to let it bother you, Tim. Please.' Mum shook her head. 'I'll sign the report card this time. And don't mention anything to Dad, especially not now with the war crimes trial coming up at the end of June.' Mum looked down and sighed. 'Dad's having such a hard time.'

'Why is the trial in June, Mum? When I arrived Dad said he wouldn't have to go to court to give evidence until later in the year.'

'We all thought that, Tim,' Mum shook her head. 'But they brought the case forward. Remember? Almost at the same time you arrived, Lord Jowitt came over from England to visit with the military lawyers here in Hamburg? They have thousands and thousands of cases for trial: the Gestapo, the SS, the Leadership Corps, the Security Police. They've set up about a hundred courts and the Lord Chancellor wants to have as many individual cases cleared as soon as possible.'

Tim nodded. Now he remembered. He'd seen a report in the newspaper

Mum continued: 'It will be hard for Dad. I went to part of the Ravensbrück Concentration Camp trial early in January, soon after the girls and I arrived here. Evidence was being given against that dreadful man, Ramdohr-the-Torturer, and against Carmen Mory the woman they called The Black Angel of Death.' Mum shook her head. 'Those poor women in Ravensbrück went through the most terrible torture, night after night after night.' She sighed. 'Some of them rubbed their hands in coal and then rubbed them in their hair.'

'Why did they do that, Mum?'

'To make their hair look dark, Tim, so they'd appear as young as possible. You see, many had turned white with terror and fatigue and knew they'd be sent to the death camps for human experiments.' Mum shook her head. 'I'll never forget Sylvia Salveson, the Norwegian lady. It must have been so hard for her to give evidence, to relive those times, to see her torturer in front of her again.'

'It will be like that for Dad, won't it, Mum?'

'Yes Tim. When they brought the trial date forward it was a great shock for your father.' Mum's lips were pressed tightly together in an angry line. 'That SS officer has so much to answer for, besides the torture that Dad and that old man went through.'

'The old man was a teacher, Mum wasn't he?'

'The old man? Yes, a professor of English at the university.' Mum nodded. 'Hitler hated England so much he had the Nazis destroy any books in English or about England. They held huge burning sessions, but it didn't do much good; people hid books they wanted to keep. The strongest opposition to Hitler was here in Hamburg.'

'You mean there were Germans who were against Hitler, Mum?'

'Of course, Tim! Don't you remember when all those generals tried to blow him up?'

Tim nodded. He'd forgotten that.

'Anyway,' said Mum. 'They can't find the old man, so that he can give evidence.' She sighed. 'I doubt if they ever will. And the notebook went missing too.'

'What notebook, Mum?'

'Oh! Don't you know about that either?'

Tim shook his head. 'I don't know very much at all, Mum.'

'Well.' Mum brushed a lock of hair back from her forehead. 'It's not something we often talk about. Naturally, it upsets Dad. But a notebook was found at the SS camp where Dad was held. It was on a bonfire, partially burned. The SS tried to get rid of a lot of evidence. This notebook and several others belonged to the man who tortured Dad.'

'What was in it, Mum?'

'It was like a diary, Tim.' Mum breathed in deeply, 'a terrible diary! That swine had recorded details of the tortures he performed, the way his victims cried out, the wounds he'd inflicted.'

Tim clenched his fists. How could anybody do that?

Mum was continuing: 'Some of the notebooks were totally destroyed; no one will ever know what disgusting crimes, what sadistic thoughts were recorded in them.

But some were recovered before they burned, when our troops entered the camp. Then the books went missing.'

'How, Mum?' Tim shook his head. 'How did they go missing?'

'No one really knows, Tim. They were locked up with other pieces of evidence in what was meant to be a safe place.'

Tim could see tears forming in Mum's eyes.

'When the prosecutors went to review them they'd disappeared.'

'You mean someone stole them, Mum?'

Mum nodded. She pulled a handkerchief from her sleeve and dabbed her eyes. She sniffed. 'That's why Dad is such a key witness; so it's up to us to support him as much as we can.'

Tim nodded. Dad didn't need any other worries right now.

'Anyway, enough of that!' Mum held out her hand. 'Let me sign your report card, Tim. And put it away before Dad comes home.'

'Okay, Mum.'

Chapter 8

THE FRATERNIZER

It was Saturday morning once more, time for the weekly trip to the NAAFI.

'Can I go down to Pooh Corner, Mum? I haven't seen it yet.'

'I thought Heinz drove you home that way on Tuesday.'

'He did, Mum, but he wouldn't let me out of the car and we couldn't actually go down the road.'

Mum sighed. 'Good for Heinz. I've no idea why you want to see that crater. It's just a smelly hole in the ground.'

Tim shrugged. 'It's just that everyone else at school from around here has seen it. They say I must be a 'mummy's boy' not being allowed to go there.'

'Oh dear!' Mum shook her head. 'The things children say to one another.' She sighed again. 'Well, they have put up barricades now; it's safe enough if you stay behind them.' She looked directly at Tim. 'Promise me you'll stay behind the barricades, and be back here in twenty minutes; we're off to the NAAFI at half past ten.'

'I know, Mum. Thanks.'

'And don't touch anything. Don't pick anything up!'

'I won't, Mum.'

It only took a few minutes to reach the crater. Tim ran down Gustav Strasse, turned left onto Klein Flottbeker Weg and right onto Schulhaus Strasse; here the smell was really strong and he slowed to a walk. Fifty yards down the road was a white painted wooden barricade.

It was quiet on the street. On the left was an orchard; small green apples already formed on the branches. And there was the cemetery Dad had mentioned; toppled gravestones littered the ground like cards spread over a green felt tabletop. In the near corner farthest from the crater was a large moss-covered table tomb. Tim shivered and hurried on.

Tim leaned on the barricade. The wood wasn't actually painted; it was white-washed with lime; it felt chalky. He looked down. Some of the white-wash had rubbed off onto his coat; he brushed it off with his hand.

The smell from the crater was bad, even this early in the morning. Tim decided that a quick look would be enough. The hole was the width of the road and about twenty feet long. The part of the sewer he could see, at the far end of the crater, was like a tunnel. It was lined with white tiles. Along one side was a raised section, like a walkway. Trickling down the middle was a steady stream of muddy-grey liquid. Tim felt sick. That was what had shot up into his bath!

Just beyond the crater were two houses. One had to be Reggie Welch's house. A shiny black Mercedes was parked in the driveway. Storks had built a nest on the roof of the other house; but that wasn't what attracted Tim, it was sudden movement at the side of the nearest house.

A voice shouted: 'Thief! Thief!'

Tim knew that voice. It was Reggie Welch. Where was he?

A loud clatter was followed by the crash of metal on concrete. A short figure carrying a grubby cloth bag came running awkwardly down the driveway. It was the boy with the close-cropped dark hair. There was a look of terror on his pale, thin face. His face was dirty, but the dark shadows beneath his blue eyes made them prominent against his sallow skin. He glanced behind him as he ran and turned, unseeing, towards Tim. Behind the boy ran Reggie Welch, his face red, heavy legs pumping up and down, waving his arms. He looked surprised to see Tim by the crater.

'Stop him!' shouted Reggie. 'Stop that thief! He's been stealing food from our dustbin.'

Stealing from a dustbin? Tim wasn't sure that taking food that had been thrown out as garbage was actually stealing. And who would do that anyway, only someone who was starving, who was desperately hungry. He remembered his own hunger at boarding school.

'Stop him!' screamed Welch.

As the boy scrambled over the barricade Tim saw that he was very thin. His bony knees seemed too large for the rest of his legs. He saw Tim and was about to turn aside when Tim slowly shook his head and winked. The boy looked surprised but then ran along the side of the crater. Reggie Welch was climbing over the whitewashed wood fence. The boy took a last look behind him then ran on past Tim. As he did so one of his sandals fell off. For a moment he hesitated, then ran over the rubble, round the other side and into the cemetery.

Quickly, Tim bent down, leaning through the whitewashed bars, and picked up the sandal. The sole was made of straw and the bindings of strips of cloth. He was about to throw it away when Welch came running up, panting. He bent down and picked up a piece of rubble.

'Yah!' Welch screamed and hurled the piece of rubble after the boy; with a dull thud it hit the mossy side of the table tomb and fell to the ground.

'You idiot!' Welch whirled round to face Tim. 'Why didn't you stop him?' He had difficulty talking as he struggled for breath.

'My mum said not to go inside the barricade.'

'Huh!' Welch's close-set, pale blue-grey eyes took on a mean look. 'What are you, a 'mummy's boy'? Or have you got a screw loose, bonkers like your dad?' He put a finger to his temple and made a twisting motion.

Tim felt the muscles of his face grow taut. What did Welch mean, saying Dad was mad? He took a step forward. 'Why, you …'

'Reggie! Reggie!' A lady with her hair in curlers came running out from behind the Mercedes. 'Reggie! Oh, there you are. Get out of there and come back here at once!'

Welch looked at Tim, a smirk on his face. 'You're nothing but a rotten fraternizer,' he said, kicking a piece of brick at Tim as he turned. 'A crazy, mad fraternizer!' he shouted as he ran off.

Tim clenched his fists, breathing hard. He so wanted to hit Reggie Welch. What did he mean saying that about Dad? As he clenched his right hand Tim felt his nails digging into something. He looked down. Of course, the straw sandal! He was about to throw it away when he stopped. He looked towards the cemetery. All was silent. Nothing moved, but instinctively he moved towards it and, looking round placed the sandal on the table tomb.

He walked slowly back down Schulhaus Strasse. As he reached Klein Flottbeker Weg he turned and looked back. The boy was seated on the ground tying on the straw sandal. He looked up. Tim waved.

Chapter 9
COMPASS NEEDLE

Tim decided not to tell Mum or Dad about the incident with Reggie Welch. Dad had said to avoid Welch, and although it wasn't Tim's fault that he'd met him at the crater he didn't want to talk about it. Welch had called him a fraternizer and Dad had said specifically not to fraternize with the enemy. But, was saving the German boy from that bully Welch fraternizing? Tim didn't think so, not when the boy was so hungry that he took scraps of food from a dustbin! He didn't want to ask now. But he was really troubled by Reggie Welch saying Dad was crazy, a mental case; he'd said it once at school too.

Dad was preoccupied with the coming trial, becoming quieter, more like when he'd first returned to England early in 1945. He was short-tempered, constantly rubbing his fingertips; and the white streak through his hair seemed more prominent because he didn't always keep it combed. He was growing thin, the skin of his face taut over his cheekbones. Mum tried to get him to eat but he often snapped at her, eating only half his food. And when Tim tried to talk to him he seemed not to hear, or appeared angry.

One morning, almost a week after Reggie Welch had called him a fraternizer Tim was in the basement cleaning his shoes for school. Dad was in the basement too, chatting with Mr. Kotsko the gardener. Mr. Kotsko had just arrived on his bicycle, a rickety old machine made up from parts he'd scrounged. Dad had found him new tyres and inner tubes to replace the old tyres that he'd filled with cloth. Mr. Kotsko wasn't German; he was Polish, a Displaced Person. He lived with other DPs in a Nissen hut with a curved, corrugated metal roof and sides, in a temporary camp near the Altona station. Mum pointed out the camp one day on the way to the NAAFI. The curved, tunnel-shaped Nissen huts reminded Tim of the Anderson shelter in their back garden in London, only the Nissen hut was much larger and was above ground. Tim still remembered being buried when the shelter collapsed when the bomb exploded. Mr. Kotsko said that black market gangs controlled the camp; nobody could do anything about it.

Tim hadn't known Mr. Kotsko was Polish until two days ago. He was trying to learn German like Sarah and baby Jane and he'd tried to speak German to Mr. Kotsko.

'I'm not German, Mr. Tim. I'm Polish.'

'Oh! I'm sorry, Mr. Kotsko.'

'Do not be sorry, Mr. Tim. But please you speak me in English. I like practice. I go to United States of America. I have applied for visa.'

'But why don't you go home to Poland?'

The gardener shook his head. 'I was brought here to work five years ago. That was bad. But then I heard all my family is dead.'

'I'm sorry,' said Tim.

The gardener nodded. 'Now my country is occupied by Russians. And what is there?' He shrugged. 'Nothing! Warsaw? It is totally destroyed. The Russians, they wait outside while the Nazis burn it to the ground.' He shook his head. 'There is nothing to go back to. I don't know where is my friends, even if they live. They probably DPs like me.'

'I see.' Tim had heard that conditions in the Russian zone of Germany were terrible. It was probably the same in Poland. 'But don't you ever want to go back?'

The gardener shrugged. 'No,' he said. 'I rather go to United States. I be free person, new life. Everywhere here destroyed. Hitler! He destroy everything.'

Tim thought about this as he polished the toe-cap of his right shoe. He was trying to make it shine like Heinz made Dad's shoes shine. Mr. Kotsko was right. Hitler had brought destruction everywhere he went. Now Germany was destroyed, Berlin was divided and Hamburg in ruins.

Heinz entered the basement from the back garden. He was dressed in uniform, a Wermacht soldiers' uniform but no longer grey; it had been dyed a very dark brown. He pressed it every day and the creases in his trousers were like a razor edge. The military buttons had been replaced with buttons made from walnut. Heinz polished them to a deep, shiny dark brown. He was smiling and whistling happily as he took off his cap.

Dad, his face contorted in anger, whirled round as Heinz closed the door. 'Stop that!' Dad's voice was low, barely above a whisper, but it was clear and biting. He was shaking. 'Stop that!'

Heinz stopped whistling. His face went white. He almost cringed. 'I am sorry, Mein Herr.' He dropped his cap and stooped to pick it up, fumbling as he did so. 'I'm so sorry, Mein Herr. I forgot.' He looked at Dad, his eyes pleading.

The skin on Dad's face was tight, ashen, stretched taut over the bones beneath. His lips were quivering and his shoulders drooped, hunched forward. He was breathing rapidly, his hands shaking as he rubbed the fingertips. He shook his head, speaking slowly:

'I asked you never to whistle that tune.' Dad's voice was now almost a whisper. He looked sideways at Heinz, his eyes half closed, squinting. He seemed to have difficulty speaking, his jaw moving up and down as if mechanically controlled.

Heinz shook his head. The dark brown cap was a twisted ball in his hands, the shiny black peak folded and cracked. He looked down. 'Please, mein Herr. Bitte. I beg forgiveness.'

Dad shut his eyes and breathed slowly and deeply.

'What is happening?' Mum was at the top of the stairs. 'Is everything all right? Will, are you all right?' She came hurrying down the stairs, her shoes clattering on the wooden steps. 'What's going on?'

Mum looked from Dad to Heinz, to Mr. Kotsko. Dad was staring at the floor, his hands constantly moving as he rubbed the finger tips.

Tim looked round. Someone had to say something. 'Heinz was whistling, Mum.'

'Oh, no!' Mum shook her head. 'Not that tune?' She went to Dad and put her arms round him.

Heinz stood twisting the cap in his hands.

'Has Dad forgiven Heinz, Mum?'

'Yes, Tim.' Mum nodded. 'Actually, your father and Heinz get on very well. Heinz was an army engineer, like Dad. He helped Dad when he was first here, when Dad was defusing unexploded bombs.' Mum shook her head. 'He hasn't whistled that tune for months.'

'What tune is it, Mum?'

'It's a theme from an opera by Wagner, Tim, a famous German composer, Hitler's favorite I believe. I think the opera is called The Valkerie. The SS officer whistled it every night before he began to torture anyone. Night after night after night he'd strut around in his shiny, polished, black jack-boots and black uniform, the Nazi swastika standing out jet black on the red armband. Dad said that after a while he could feel the pain of the torture to come even before it began.' Mum had tears in her eyes. 'Even if they didn't torture him on a particular night, just the sound of that tune being whistled brought pain.'

Tim shuddered. The SS officer was a demon from hell. When Dad was wounded in Italy in 1944, Sergeant Morse had stayed with him. The German troops had counter-attacked. Dad and Sergeant Morse were trapped behind enemy lines. They were lucky not to be discovered. But, in order to avoid being found the sergeant had to move Dad, carrying him further and further behind enemy lines as the Allied army renewed their attack and the enemy retreated north towards Rome. Dad became ill; the lack of proper medical attention and the constant moving prevented his wounds from healing. Mum said it was lucky he didn't lose his leg. Eventually Dad and Sergeant Morse were caught at a farm where they'd taken refuge.

'If that farmer hadn't given Dad and Sergeant Morse away, Dad wouldn't have been tortured, would he, Mum?'

Mum nodded. 'Probably not, Tim. But sometimes things work out for the best. If they hadn't been betrayed Dad wouldn't have been taken to the German military hospital in Rome. He's never forgotten the wonderful treatment he received there. He believes the German army doctor saved his life.'

'That's why he was able to escape, wasn't it.'

'That's right, Tim. But his leg hadn't fully healed.' Mum shook her head. 'And he had to steal some clothes as his own uniform had been taken away. All he could find was a German uniform.'

Tim remembered Dad telling him how he'd sneaked away from the hospital one night and hidden in a nearby railway yard. It was pouring with rain so he took shelter in a shed. He dropped off to sleep and awoke to the sounds of shouted orders. The yard was full of German soldiers guarding British and American prisoners of war.

'It was because he had the German uniform that he was tortured, wasn't it, Mum?'

Mum nodded. 'That's right, Tim. They caught him as he tried to sneak away. He was accused of being a spy.'

'And he saw Sergeant Morse among the prisoners in the railway yard, and those other men.'

Again Mum nodded. 'That's why he knew they were alive and could pass a message on to the Resistance after he escaped the second time.' Mum sighed. 'It was so ironic. Three days later our troops captured Rome. By that time Dad was on a train to Germany, but not to a prisoner of war camp like the other POWs. He was taken to the SS camp.'

'Did the torture make Dad go mad, Mum?'

There was silence. Then Mum spoke again. 'It's a wonder your father didn't go mad, Tim. Some poor souls did. The SS officer played on Dad's unhealed wound. When he tired of that he mutilated Dad's hands. He accused Dad of being a spy, an undercover agent from the Special Operations Executive. That was his excuse for the torture, even though Dad still wore his dog tag with his army number stamped on it.'

There were tears in Mum's eyes. As she pulled a handkerchief from the pocket in her apron the keys on her belt jangled. 'No torture is excusable, and Dad was a wounded soldier, not a member of the S.O.E.' She shook her head. 'He had a nervous breakdown; that's why he was in hospital in England all those months.'

'But he didn't go mad, Mum! Did he? He didn't go crazy or anything?'

'Tim. What is this?' Mum dabbed her eyes and peered down at him. 'What is this about Dad being mad? Now, tell me.'

'Reggie Welch said Dad is a mental case.'

'Why … the …' Mum screwed up her handkerchief. 'The young …'

*   *   *

The steady thump, thump, thump of Welch kicking his chair was driving Tim crazy. The more he tried to ignore it the more Welch seemed to enjoy it. It wasn't true that if you ignored someone like Welch they'd get fed up and stop!

The thump-thump continued. Mr. Morgan looked directly at Tim just as he was about to turn and tell Welch to stop it. He put his head down and concentrated on the algebraic equation in his exercise book. The thumping stopped. Good! Then he felt a searing pain in his buttocks where the scar of a carbuncle he'd had at boarding school was barely healed.

'Agh!' Tim stifled the cry of pain. He looked up to see if the teacher was staring at him. No. He was writing another problem on the blackboard.

Again pain shot through Tim's behind. He whirled round in his seat just in time to see Reggie Welch bend down and remove a compass needle from the welt of his heavy brown leather boots.

As the bully straightened up Tim clenched his left fist in a tight ball and lashed out. Welch was surprised, his mouth half open as Tim's fist hit his lower lip. He cried out, his pale grey-blue eyes screwed up in pain. Then his hands came up and he pressed them over his mouth. The compass needle dropped to the floor and rolled under the radiator along the wall. As Welch started to moan, swaying slowly from side to side, Tim saw a trickle of blood ooze down Reggie's chin and drip onto his shirt.

Chapter 10

LIKE FATHER, LIKE SON

Heinz was driving Dad and Tim home. Tim sat huddled in the back of the khaki-coloured Volkswagen, his behind really painful from the caning he'd received from Mr. Morgan; and his back ached too. Friday the thirteenth of June. What a horrible day it had been.

'Don't argue with me, Athelstan! Bend over.' The teacher had flexed the cane, bending it back and forth as he spoke. Behind the thick-lensed glasses his eyes narrowed.

'But, sir, he ...'

'Quiet!' Mr. Morgan brushed a wisp of greasy hair from left to right across his head. 'Quiet! Bend over or you'll receive twelve strokes, not six.'

It was useless. Tim leaned over the back of the chair and grasped either side of the seat. Looking sideways and to his left he saw the teacher move his feet into position.

Crack! Tim wasn't ready. Almost before he heard the whistle of the cane through the air he felt the searing pain. He clenched his teeth and stifled the cry rising in his throat.

'One,' said the teacher.

Crack! This time Tim heard the whistle of the cane and tensed his muscles. It seemed to make the pain worse.

'Two.'

As he tried to relax, closing his eyes, Tim heard the whistle of the cane slicing through the air; then he felt searing pain as the cane rippled up his back. What was happening?

'Missed,' said Mr. Morgan. 'Missed. That one doesn't count, Athelstan.'

Tim felt his legs tremble uncontrollably. He wanted to pee but hung on grimly.

Now, hunched up in the back of the car, Tim recalled the beating; he couldn't help it as the Volkswagen had poor springs and every bump in the road, however small, sent shudders through the small vehicle and through the hard seat. Even though he knew Heinz wasn't aiming to hit every pothole it felt like it.

Dad, very quiet now, sat to the right of Heinz who looked straight ahead saying nothing. Heinz was usually very talkative.

Mr. Morgan hadn't allowed Tim to say a word, hadn't allowed him to explain about the compass needle, or the scars from his carbuncles. Reggie Welch, moaning and sniffling, had been taken to the sick room. Then Tim was marched down the corridor, down the stairs to the office. He still hadn't been allowed to say a word about what Welch had done and was told to wait.

It was while he stood waiting, wondering what was
going to happen, if he would get the cane, that he heard
a car screech to a halt outside the front of the school.
Heavy feet ran up the stone steps and then down the
corridor. The office door burst open.

'Where is he? Where's my boy?'

A short, heavily built man with straight fair hair
plastered down with hair cream glared round the office.
His head was thrust forward aggressively. 'Where is he?'
The man wore a smooth, serge cloth khaki uniform with
the green CCG flash sewn on each shoulder. It had to
be Mr. Welch. He looked straight at Tim with blue-grey
eyes half hidden through lowered lids as he ignored the
secretary trying to direct him to the sick room. He took
a step towards Tim.

Tim flinched and pressed himself against the office
wall, feeling threatened by the unblinking stare from the
pale eyes beneath fair, almost white eyebrows.

'You're the one, aren't you? Athelstan's boy! Mad!
Crazy!' Mr. Welch sneered, thin lips drawn back. 'Like
father, like son, I'd say.' Then he turned slowly on his heel,
eyes still fixed on Tim as he followed the directions given
by the secretary who now stood by the door, holding it
open for him.

It was then that Mr. Morgan returned with the long,
thin, Malacca cane. He had pushed up first the left, then
the right sleeve of his brown wool cardigan, revealing
thin hairy arms and bony elbows.

Dad hadn't stopped since they'd arrived at Gustav Strasse
Sieben.

'To be called from my office in the middle of the afternoon, and have to stand there and take insult after insult from that smarmy little …' Dad glared across the dining table. 'Seven stitches!' He shook his head. 'The boy will have a nasty scar. 'Perhaps we should…' Dad looked at Tim. 'Either Mum or I have to go back to England for a few days, to settle the damage claim for our Hamstead house with the War Claims people. If the trial is over by then I'll go; and I've a good mind to take you back with me and go down and see the headmaster and see if he'll take you back.'

Tim's throat tightened. He felt like crying, but that would only make things worse.

'Oh, no!' Mum shook her head. 'I don't think that's the answer, Will. Tim's only just getting over the poor food at that school. Look how ill he was. Anyway, I believe Tim.'

Tim looked from one to the other. Mum believed him. Would Dad agree? For some reason he didn't think so. Why wasn't Dad taking his side, sticking up for him instead of Welch? Welch was the bully; he'd started it. And Dad had said Welch was a problem.

'Well! All this over a pin prick! A mere pin prick!' Dad shook his head. 'The number of times I was jabbed with a pin at school, or sat on a drawing pin someone put on my seat.'

'It wasn't a pin, Dad. It was a compass needle stuck in his boot. And he kicked as hard as he could. It really hurt. And it was right next to that carbuncle scar. And it wasn't once. He did it twice.' Surely Dad could understand how painful that was?

'Once, twice, what does it matter? You must have done something to annoy him.'

Tim was speechless. How could he explain? He couldn't tell Dad about the morning at the sewer crater, or then Dad might find out about Welch calling him a fraternizer. So he couldn't even tell Dad that Welch said he was bonkers and had a screw loose and was mad.

Tim saw Sarah appear in the doorway. She stood still, waiting to say goodnight, but neither Mum nor Dad noticed her. Her face was sad, her brown eyes serious as she listened intently.

Dad was rubbing the ends of his fingers. 'I can't have this sort of thing, Tim. I won't have it! That Welch character won't let this rest, you know; he'll keep bringing it up. You must stop being so aggressive.' He shook his head. 'It makes me wonder about that other boy, during the war, the one in Medbury. What was it? Two ribs broken?'

Tim couldn't believe his ears. It was getting worse. The other boy was Chalky White. Chalky and the other boys had been bullying Sarah; he'd had to act fast and the only thing to do was charge at Chalky, put him off balance, grab Sarah and pull her after him. It was an accident that his elbow jabbed Chalky in the ribs. And anyway, before Dad had left on the troop ship for Italy he'd said: 'Look after Mum and Sarah for me, Tim.' And that's what he was doing, protecting Sarah.

Sarah's voice cut through the silence. She spoke very slowly and clearly. 'Tim was rescuing me from Chalky White, Dad.' She stood hands on hips, looking very serious. 'Chalky was a bully. Tim rescued me.'

Dad seemed startled by the sudden interruption. 'Please don't interrupt, Sarah.' He turned, looking over his shoulder. 'Isn't it your bedtime?'

Sarah nodded, saying nothing. She looked at Tim.

Tim wished he could go to bed. The seat of the dining room chair wasn't upholstered and he was very uncomfortable; he thought he could feel each individual welt from the caning.

Mum got up from the table. 'Come along, Sarah. Say goodnight to Dad and I'll tuck you into bed.'

It was quiet in the house. Nobody was awake yet. Tim lay in bed thinking. He hadn't really slept all night, worrying about school and what had happened yesterday. He wasn't usually superstitious, but this Friday the thirteenth had been a terrible day. He'd been in Germany less than a month and look at the trouble he was in. Like father, like son! If someone had said that to him two years ago he'd have been so proud. Maybe it really would be better if he was back in England. Maybe, with all the worries Dad had, it would be better if he was back at the boarding school. The summer term would end soon and if he was in England he could stay with Grandpa George and Grandma Rose for the holidays. That wouldn't be so bad.

He took his pocket watch from the bedside table. He could barely see the hands; almost six o'clock. The sun was still below the horizon and only just lightening the sky; it wouldn't be up for another hour or so. That was the trouble with Double Summer Time: putting the clock ahead so the evenings were long and the farmers could get a lot of work done made it so dark in the morning.

Mum said they were going to end Double Summer Time in Germany at the end of the month. With the poor food rations the German workers complained that they couldn't work the longer days.

But Germany wasn't the only place short of food. The weather was bad all over Europe, the heat, the drought. Just last week, in London, over a thousand British housewives had stormed the Houses of Parliament. There were pictures in the papers of women holding up banners: 'MORE FOOD!' 'OUR CHILDREN NEED FOOD!' And the papers said that if the drought continued the potato harvest would be disastrous.

Tim turned on his side, trying to get comfortable. His behind was still painful and his back ached where the cane had run up his backbone. 'Missed!' Tim thought Mr. Morgan enjoyed caning. He hadn't told Mum or Dad about Mr. Morgan missing, or about how badly it had hurt when the cane hit a carbuncle scar. It was bad enough getting the cane without reminding everyone. He tried lying on the other side; it was no good, he might as well get up. He stretched and walked slowly to the window, breathing in deeply. His metal trunk was no longer there; Heinz had taken it to the basement, to the air raid shelter. He shrugged and peered out at the dawn. Perhaps he'd be re-packing the trunk soon?

Beyond the beechnut hedge the fields were silent. Nothing stirred, except... What was that, in the potato field? Was it that boy again? Tim was sure it was the boy even though he could only see a shadowy silhouette against the lightening sky. He'd seen the boy three times before, this was the fourth; and his run was unmistakable. Over the boy's shoulder Tim could see what looked like his bag. Close behind was another shadow, quite large. It was a dog. Then Tim saw a third shadowy figure, a man, tall and thin, a stick raised above his head, running fast and gaining on the boy.

The dog turned and Tim heard a deep, throaty growl, faint on the morning air. As the man drew near the dog jumped. The stick came down but the dog's jaw locked on the man's wrist. All the movements seemed to be in slow motion, grey colourless shapes moving in the dawn shadows. There was a cry of rage as the man and dog fell to the ground. The boy stopped and turned for an instant before running on.

The man was now on his knees and Tim saw him reach with his free hand and grasp the stick. He raised it high above his head and brought it down on the dog's back. There was a piercing howl of pain repeated as the stick crashed down again and again.

Without realizing what he was doing, Tim opened his window. He leaned out, shouting, 'No! No! Stop that!'

The man got up and turned, looking towards the house, slapping the stick against his calf. The dog lay on the ground, unmoving.

'Leave it alone!' Tim shouted at the top of his voice. He looked left and right. There was no sign of the boy. 'Leave it alone!'

Behind Tim there was a clicking sound and the light came on in his bedroom.

'Tim! What's the matter?' Mum hurried into the room. 'Are you having a nightmare?'

'No, Mum.' Tim turned round. 'There's a man out there beating a dog. I think it might be dead.'

Chapter 11

THE ESCAPE

'Where is the dog, Tim?'

'It should be around here, Dad. I'm pretty sure this is the place. I could see it from my bedroom.' Anxiously, Tim searched the edge of the potato field. It was almost daylight now. Where was the dog? Was it alive? Had it run off?

'Sh!' Dad held up his hand. 'I can hear something. Over there!'

Tim heard a faint whimper, somewhere to his right. He started to run.

'Slow down, son!' called Dad. 'An injured animal can be very dangerous.'

Tim stopped, waiting until Dad caught up with him; then, after only a few more steps they found the dog, half-hidden in a furrow between two rows of potato plants. Its coat was dull, but the short hair was a beautiful chestnut brown. It struggled to get up, whimpering as it did so.

'Steady on, old fellow.' Dad approached slowly and squatted down. He held out his hand, back towards the flat, snubbed snout of the dog. 'Beautiful animal,' he said. 'A Boxer. The German police use them.'

The dog was quiet now, sniffing Dad's hand. Dad knelt beside it. It started to lick the back of his hand. Tim looked out across the field, searching left and right, then back the way they'd come. All was still. There was no sign of either the man or the boy.

'Poor old fellow.' Dad stroked the dog's head and gently scratched between its ears. 'There. There.'

'Do you think it understands you, Dad?'

'Not the words, Tim.' Dad shook his head. 'But it understands the tone of voice. It knows we're not a threat. Here! You stroke him while I see if he's injured.' Dad took Tim's hand and brought it carefully to the flat snout. The Boxer sniffed and then licked Tim's hand with a warm, soft tongue.

'There. There.' said Tim, copying Dad's soothing tone. 'We'll look after you.'

The dog blinked as Tim scratched its head. Then it moved, craning its head back over its shoulder to where Dad was feeling its back legs. Slowly Dad moved his hands up and over its hindquarters, past the short, stubby tail and along its back. As he did so the dog started to whimper and take short sharp gulps of air, its tongue lolling out.

'Something there.' Dad looked up. 'Let's hope its only bruising.' He continued to probe, sliding his hands gently forward over the dog's coat. It whimpered as Dad's nail-less fingers moved to its ribs. 'Hm.' Dad nodded, then moved forward.

Tim could feel the dog become tense, restless. 'I think he may have hurt his front legs, Dad.'

The Boxer yelped as Dad touched its left front leg.
'Definitely something there.' Dad raised his hand. It
was bloody. He tried to lift the dog by its shoulders. It
whimpered and then gave a low, warning growl. Dad
nodded.

'Go back to the house, Tim. Get a blanket. There are
some old grey ones in the basement, in the cupboard on
your left as you go into the shelter. We'll roll him onto
a blanket and carry him that way, like a stretcher. And
tell Mum we'll be back to do some first aid.' There was
a change in Dad's voice, a lift that hadn't been there for a
long time. 'Off you go, old chap!'

Tim jumped up and started to run for the house. 'Back
in a minute, Dad!'

'Right. That looks fine, Major Athelstan.' The army
veterinary officer stood back from the work bench in
the basement and smiled. 'Lucky your son saw what was
happening. With this broken leg the poor animal would
have been unable to move. And look how thin it is; it's
half-starved. No knowing how long it would have lasted
in that condition.'

Tim looked at the dog. When they'd brought the Boxer
into the basement it was obvious from the way the leg was
bent that it was broken. And what the vet said was true:
you could see every one of the Boxer's ribs beneath the
dull chestnut coat.

But before that, on his way from the house with the
blanket, Tim thought he'd broken his own leg. He was
close to Dad, running along the edge of the field behind
the Beechnut hedge when he felt a tug at his right foot
and a sudden, sharp pain round his ankle. He stumbled

and fell, twisting his right leg under him as he did so and landing heavily on his behind.

'Ouch!' Tim rolled over, carefully stretching out his leg. It wasn't broken.

'Are you all right, Tim?' Dad shouted.

'Something tripped me, Dad.' Tim sat up. 'Ouch!' He breathed in sharply through his teeth. Falling like that had made the welts on his behind ache and throb again. Carefully he shifted position and stared down at his feet. Wrapped tightly round his left ankle was a length of wire, attached to which was a stick about a foot long. The stick had a pointed end.

'What do you mean, something tripped you?'

Tim was carefully loosening the wire. It was quite thin, made from several thinner strands twisted together, like the wire to hang pictures. It looked like brass but was dull, and it wasn't actually wrapped round his ankle but formed in a noose. The noose was tight. Finally he got it off and held it up, rubbing his ankle with his free hand.

'This was round my ankle. It's a snare, isn't it, Dad?' Tim got up carefully. His leg hurt but it wasn't too bad. He picked up the grey blanket and handed Dad the wire noose.

'Hm!' Dad took the wire. 'Are you all right?'

'Yes, Dad, I'm fine.' Tim shifted his weight off his right leg.

'Are you sure?'

'Yes, Dad. I twisted my leg a bit, that's all.'

Dad looked at the wire noose. 'It's a rabbit snare alright; someone obviously set it to catch their dinner.'

Tim nodded. 'Mr. Runciman showed me how to set a snare.'

'Mr. Runciman?'

'The beekeeper, Dad, at Medbury.'

'Ah, yes. I remember now. Mum said he would bring you a rabbit or two sometimes.'

'Usually just one, Dad.' Tim nodded, remembering those delicious rabbit stews during the war. He could almost taste the juices and the gravy. During the war food rationing had been much worse than it was now and he'd always been hungry. Mr. Runciman's rabbits had been very welcome. He thought about the German boy, how thin he was; perhaps he'd set the snare. Or maybe the man had set it, had caught a rabbit and then found the boy stealing it. No, that couldn't be right, otherwise Tim wouldn't have caught his foot in it; the snare was still set.

Dad was speaking: 'He was a bit of a poacher, was he, old Mr. Runciman?'

Tim nodded. 'Yes, he was, Dad. But he was an expert. He showed me how to make snares and how to bury them for a day before setting them so that the rabbits wouldn't smell the scent from my hands. He buried his gloves too, so they wouldn't smell when he set snares along the trail.'

'Ah! So you're a poacher too, are you, Tim?' Dad was smiling.

'Not exactly, Dad. I know how to do it, but I know it's illegal.'

Dad chuckled. 'One of these days when we're back in England I'll show you a couple of tricks.'

Tim stared at his father. 'Do you mean... are you a poacher, Dad?'

Dad shook his head, laughing. 'I wouldn't say that, Tim, but like you I learned a few tricks when I was a boy.

Anyway, let's have that blanket and get this wounded soldier up to the house.'

'Can we keep him, Dad? Mum?' Tim looked from one to the other.

'Well, we don't know who he belongs to, Tim.' Dad shrugged. 'He doesn't have a collar or tag or anything like that. But he is a beautiful animal, even if he does look half-starved, so someone is bound to search for him. However, what we can do is look after him until that leg heals.'

'And we can feed him, right, Dad?' Sarah clapped her hands. 'And we can make him fat.'

Tim felt a little annoyed that Sarah was butting in. He'd seen the dog being attacked. He'd found the dog with Dad and helped bring him home. And he couldn't help thinking about Bits; ever since Bits had died during the war he'd always wanted a dog.

'I don't know about making him fat.' Mum smiled. 'It's difficult enough feeding this family, even though the weekly rations are better for us here than in England.'

'He can eat the scraps,' said Sarah.

'Yes. He can eat scraps,' said baby Jane, a very serious look on her face. With her serious look, wavy brown hair and blue eyes she looked like Mum.

Dad laughed. 'What scraps? You children always clean your plates. I don't see any scraps there.'

Tim looked round the table. It was true, they always ate everything; it was a wartime habit, never to leave anything, even fat. 'I can leave some, Dad. We could all leave something.'

Mum shook her head. 'Don't worry about that, Tim. I'll sort something out. The dog will be fed.'

Just then Inge came into the room. 'Excuse me, sir. A man comes to see you. I leave him in hall.'

Tim's heart sank. The dog's owner had come to claim him. Why now? This had been the best Saturday since he'd arrived in Germany. And he knew, even though Dad hadn't said so, that Dad would like to have the Boxer stay with them; he knew by the way Dad handled the dog, the way he spoke to it. The Boxer was nothing like Bits, but Tim could see it would be good for Dad to have a dog again.

'Who is this man, Inge?' Dad pushed his chair back.

'He is army man. He comes on…' Inge moved her hands, as if revving up a motorcycle.

'A motorcycle?' said Dad. 'A dispatch-rider? Hm. That's odd. It must be important to come round on a Saturday evening.' He stood up. 'I'll see what he wants.' He opened the door to the lounge and strode through, heading towards the door to the hallway. He closed the door behind him.

There was the sound of muffled voices. Gradually Dad's voice grew louder until he was almost shouting.

'Escaped!' Dad's voice was raised in anger. 'They let that swine escape? Damn it! How could they?'

Tim looked across at Mum.

Chapter 12

TO SWIM OR NOT TO SWIM

Ever since the news that the SS officer has escaped, Gustav Strasse Sieben had been very quiet. Dad didn't want to speak to anyone, except Mum.

On Sunday, Dad spent much of his time in the garden, tending his cucumbers, tomatoes and marrows. Because of the extreme cold of the past winter there were few bees to pollinate the plants, so Dad went round with a very small camel-hair paint brush distributing pollen from one flower to another.

'It's best to leave Dad alone at present, Tim,' said Mum. 'Don't bother him. The peace of the garden does him good.'

Tim nodded. 'I know, Mum. But I still can't believe it, letting that SS officer escape. I hope they catch him soon.'

'So do I.' Mum sighed. 'Immediately they found that he was gone they sent patrols out to Langenhorn.'

'Where's that, Mum?'

'About ten miles northwest of here. There used to be a large SS barracks there.'

'But isn't that kind of obvious, Mum? Why would he go there?'

Mum nodded. 'I know what you're thinking, Tim, but sometimes the most obvious places are the best in which to hide, a place people would least expect someone to go. The man will be looking for help; he needs to lie low for a while if he hopes to escape; and he may have friends in the Langenhorn area, people who will help him.' Mum shook her head. 'There are still Nazi elements underground.'

Tim knew that. Dad had been following reports on the radio about a committee meeting in London. They said that fascism and Nazism were coming back and were growing in parts of Germany and in Argentina. Tim had even heard that some people believed that Hitler hadn't really committed suicide but had escaped to Argentina or somewhere else in South America. Dad said some people would believe anything.

'Anyway, Tim, changing the subject: I don't want to go over what happened at school again, but I'm worried.'

'But it wasn't my fault, Mum. Really.'

Mum held up her hand. 'I don't want to talk about it. I've said all along that I believe you. What I was going to say, Tim is that you should make some friends. It's not good for you to be on your own all the time.'

'Well I won't be now, Mum. I've got Bits to look after.'

Mum nodded. 'That's true, unless of course the owner claims him. And I know you've always wanted a pet. But I'm serious about finding friends. What about young Fisk?'

Tim shook his head. 'He's a friend of Reggie Welch, Mum; so is Alan Graham. Reggie gives them fountain pens and propelling pencils.'

'Mm.' Mum frowned. I don't know anyone else in this immediate area.' She paused. 'I tell you what we'll do: next weekend, while Dad's away in England dealing with the War Claims Office, we'll go to the Country Club. You haven't been there yet. Lots of families go on the weekend. There's tennis and swimming. It's good fun.'

Tennis! Tim didn't like tennis. He'd tried it at school in England, but he much preferred cricket. And swimming! He wasn't good at that either. In fact he couldn't really swim. When they stayed with Grandpa Cecil and Grandma Maud at Eastbourne and went to the beach, when he went in the sea he'd kept one toe on the sand, hopping along and splashing with his other leg to make it look as if he was swimming. He'd feel stupid at the Country Club pool; the water would be clear and everyone would see what he was doing.

But there was no getting out of it. Mum was determined he should make friends, and the Country Club was the place to do it!

'Come on Tim!' called Mum, two weeks later. 'Time to be off! I've got your swimsuit and towel.'

'Coming, Mum,' Tim shouted up the basement stairs. 'I won't be a minute.' He groaned. This was it! Now everyone would know he couldn't swim, except Dad who was still in England. The pool was indoors and was heated, and Sarah had taken lessons with Mrs. Beecher and could really swim now. And Mum said baby Jane loved floating on her back; she didn't put a toe on the bottom. It was going to be really embarrassing!

He fondled Bit's head, scratching the boxer between its ears. The decision to call the Boxer Bits was easy. They couldn't think of another name and Bits seemed to respond to the name, pricking up his short pointed ears.

'I've got to go, Bits.' Tim sighed.

The Boxer looked up from where he was lying, head cocked to one side. His eyes were dark brown, almost black, and they shone in the sunlight coming through the long narrow basement windows. Bit's left front leg was still in the plaster cast the vet had put on. The right leg was stretched out beside it.

'I don't want to go,' said Tim. 'But I have to.' He shook his head. 'So you be good and don't keep getting up. Don't try to follow me.'

That had become a problem. Except for his broken leg Bits had recovered quickly from the beating he'd taken. And he'd learned to get up and limp around on three legs. Before Dad left for England he'd brought home a thick leather collar. It was black with shiny metal studs; and he'd made a lead from a length of rope and a shackle on a swivel he'd found in the basement. Each evening, before he left, Dad walked Bits slowly round the garden. Tim walked alongside. Not a word was spoken. It was peaceful. But Bits didn't like being left in the basement after these visits.

'Don't try to get up the stairs again, Bits. You know you can't get back down and you'll hurt yourself if you try.' Tim put his arms round Bits' neck and hugged him. 'I don't want that. I want you to get better.' The dog

FLAMES IN THE RUINS

licked his face. 'Agh!' Tim laughed and wiped his cheek with the back of his hand. The stubby tail wagged to and fro and Bits licked his chops.

'Tim! Will you please get up here! Now!'

'Coming!' Tim scrambled up from the blanket on the basement floor. He held up his hand, palm forward. 'Platz!' he said firmly to Bits. 'Platz!'

Heinz had taught him a few commands in German. They were easy to remember because they were similar to words in English. 'Sitz!' was easy to understand and 'platz' meant place. Tim was beginning to realize that quite a lot of German words were similar to English. You just had to listen carefully.

'Tim! I mean it!'

Tim thundered up the stairs. 'See you later, Bits.'

'They emptied the pool on Thursday to clean it,' said Mrs. Beecher. She shook her head. 'And when they came to fill it again on Friday they found that the chemicals needed to keep the water clean hadn't been delivered. Huh! I ask you! That Cyril Welch and his Supplies Distribution!'

Tim smiled. No swimming! Wouldn't Reggie Welch hate it if he knew his father had saved Tim. Mr. Welch would be mad too.

They were standing on the Country Club patio. Light grey stone steps between grey stone balustrades led up to a large area enclosed by a low parapet. It was paved with large rectangular flagstones that, to Tim, looked like gravestones; he could imagine names carved in the thick stone: HERE LIES THE BODY OF… He shivered.

'Are you cold, Tim?'

'No, Mum. It's just the breeze. I'm warm after the walk.' A pleasant breeze blew across the patio.

The walk from Guastav Strasse had taken only ten minutes, but the sun was hot in a clear, cloudless blue sky. They'd hurried past Pooh Corner as the heat of the day made the stench from the sewer unbearable. But, once they'd passed through the gates to the Country Club it seemed a little cooler as a tall rhododendron hedge on either side of the winding driveway gave some shade.

Halfway down the paved driveway a smaller road branched to the right, winding through thick bushes.

'That leads to the service buildings,' said Mum. 'Nothing interesting there.'

Tim was grateful for the breeze on the patio as it cleared his nose of the putrid sewer smell.

'Perfect day for swimming,' said Mrs. Beecher, shaking her head. 'And I have so many youngsters to teach.' She looked down at Sarah and Jane. 'You girls are doing very well, two of my star pupils. I was going to have you in the deep end today, Sarah,'

'Oh, dear. What a pity.' Mum sighed. 'Well, Tim, no swimming today I'm afraid, but the tennis courts are round the back, along that path to the left.' She pointed to a gravel path beyond the stone steps. 'Why don't you go and see if there's someone to have a game with.'

'That's a good idea.' Mrs. Beecher smiled. 'There are quite a few youngsters your age at the courts, Tim. You'll have fun. Tennis racquets are in the locker room.'

'Can I go, Mum?' said Sarah.

'No, dear. You and Jane stay with me. I'm sure you'd like to help me plan Jane's birthday party.'

Tim turned away quickly and ran down the steps. He didn't want to play tennis, but he certainly didn't want to get involved in planning a party. He just hoped Mum might make some jam tarts, and maybe a treacle tart too; she probably would as Sarah loved treacle tart and liked making jam tarts, cutting the small circles of pastry and filling them.

He made his way slowly along the gravel path to the corner of the main building. The gravel crunched beneath his feet. It seemed very loud. There were flowerbeds to his left, between the building and the path but they were empty, unplanted, the heavy clay soil pale and dry. On the right side of the path rose tall rhododendron bushes full of dark blooms.

It was hot. The early afternoon sun was reflected off the white bricks of the clubhouse, trapped between the building and the high bushes. Tim felt that something was missing but couldn't immediately think what. He'd not been here before so what could it be? Then he realized. There was no buzzing, no bees! With the mass of blossoms on the rhododendron the place should be swarming with bees. Dad was right, the harvest would probably be poor this year and that would be bad.

Just beyond the corner of the main clubhouse building the path divided, the left fork leading to the tennis courts Tim could hear shouts and a sudden burst of laughter. That sounded like Welch! Tim stopped. The right fork in the path, lined on either side by more rhododendrons, curved down and to the right. Where did it lead? There was another burst of laughter. It was Welch all right! Tim made a decision; he'd follow the path for short distance.

Chapter 13

FISHY BUSINESS

Tim hadn't gone far when the thick barrier of the bushes muffled the sounds from the clubhouse and tennis courts. Gradually the sounds became fainter and fainter until he could no longer hear them. It was very quiet here except for the crunch of gravel beneath his feet; it really did sound loud. He stepped onto the grass verge on his right. That was better. He walked on slowly.

After a while the path took a sharp turn to the right and there in front of him was a large area of untended grass. It would make a super cricket pitch if cut. On the far side was a large pond, the surface of the water smooth and still. Tim ran through the long grass to the water's edge. The pond was obviously man-made, or at least it had been carefully looked after. Around the edge were large rocks of the same grey stone as the clubhouse patio. Bushes and shrubs had been planted, some close to the water, others beside the overgrown gravel path that surrounded the pond.

Tim stared at the water. His shadow stretched darkly over the surface; beneath there were flashes of light, some red, some gold. The pond was full of small fish about five or six inches long. Most of them were silver-grey, but swimming among the silvery fish were some goldfish. Tim lay down on a flat rock that jutted out slightly over the water. The rock was warm from the sun but shadow was creeping over it, inching its way from a clump of bushes to the left. Tim gently stretched out his left hand and dipped it into the water. A small shoal of fish approached. Tim wiggled his fingers and they veered away sharply as if one.

He was about to get up and explore further when he became aware of a flip-flopping noise. It wasn't loud but regular, coming from the left. Instinctively Tim rolled carefully off the rock and under the bushes. He was just in time. A pair of sandal clad feet passed by. Someone was walking on the grass verge just as he had. Through the cover of the bushes Tim silently watched and waited. The German boy came into view, his bag slung over his shoulder; his sandals slapping gently against the soles of his feet.

Tim lay still, watching. What was the boy doing here? At the far end of the pond was a thick barrier of rhododendrons. Down to the left, beyond the pond, was a grey, weathered wooden gate. The boy ignored the gate and disappeared into the bushes.

Tim pushed himself up and, half-crouching ran along the grass beside the path. When he came to the spot where the boy had vanished he almost missed the narrow gap in the hedge. He carefully inched his way through. On the other side was another pond, larger than the first, surrounded by thick, high bushes. There was no path round this pond, only a narrow stretch of grass. The German boy was hurrying round the edge of the pond to the thick hedge on the far side. Once again there was a wooden gate to the left, but he ignored this and pushed his way into the bushes.

Tim followed, running quickly and silently over the grass. There was movement in the pond and he paused to take a quick look. There were masses of fish, only these were bigger, about eight to ten inches long and they were all silver-grey. He hurried on.

He was about to step out through the gap he found in the hedge when he stopped short. There was the boy not more than twenty feet away; his old cloth bag was on the ground and he was lowering himself onto the grass bank beside a third pond. He carefully lowered himself onto his stomach and slowly lowered his left arm into the water. He lay there completely still his back towards Tim. What was he doing?

Five minutes passed; ten minutes; Tim wanted to move; he was getting cramp in the calf of his right leg. But if he moved he might make a noise. The boy continued to lie on the grass, unmoving. Tim tried wiggling his toes; it helped a bit.

Slowly and carefully Tim eased his weight onto his left leg. As he did so the boy moved, his arm coming up out of the water so fast that Tim was taken by surprise. Water poured down the boy's arm as a large silver-scaled fish flew through the air twisting and turning. It landed on the grass with a thud. The boy sprang to his feet and raised a thick short stick in his right hand; he struck the fish twice on the head; it quivered and then was still and silent, gleaming silver in the sunlight. With hardly a pause the boy scooped up the fish and thrust it and the short stick into his old cloth bag.

Tim had no time to move before the boy was headed towards him, still fastening the bag. He looked up and stopped short with surprise, clasping the old cloth bag to his chest. His mouth was open, blue eyes staring at Tim. Then he ran, pushing past Tim, the straw-soled sandals flip-flopping against his feet. As he reached the far side of the second pond he turned, looking back. Tim didn't know why, but he waved.

Chapter 14

A MASTER FOR FISHING

'Heinz.'

'Yes, Mr. Tim.'

'Do you know anything about catching fish?'

'Na ja!' Heinz laughed. He steered the Volkswagen round a large pothole, then spun the wheel to avoid another. Tim peered through the windshield wondering how Heinz could see anything. Rain beat down on the glass as the wipers laboured, shuddering, barely clearing a space before it was covered yet again. But Heinz was so used to driving the route to school that he'd told Tim he could just about remember all the bumps and ruts and potholes in the unmade road that skirted the river.

It had rained very hard over night and, although the ground was crying out for moisture, the damaged drains couldn't handle the flood of surplus water. It streamed off the hard-packed soil in the nearby fields, filling the potholes and ruts, creating miniature muddy ponds and lakes.

'I am a master for fishing,' said Heinz. 'Since I am a boy.' He laughed. 'Ask me anything for fishing and I tell you.'

'How did you learn?' asked Tim.

'My uncle. He had a boat like a house.'

'A houseboat?' said Tim.

'Ja.' Heinz nodded, steering to avoid another hole. 'Ja. Ein hausboot. You say the same in English?'

'Yes.' Tim smiled. 'A houseboat.' Now he knew another German word.

The unmade road shortened the drive to school by about ten minutes, but today it was hard going. Heinz slowed right down and eased the car, rocking and swaying through a flooded area that covered the road from side to side. On the right side, between the road and the river were blackened ruins; a fast-flowing stream of water ran bubbling along what might once have been a pathway between blocks of flats.

'You ask about fishing,' said Heinz.

'Yes.' Tim turned away from the scene of the ruins. 'I saw someone lying on the ground with their arm in the water and...'

'And they pull out fish quickly?' said Heinz. 'Ja?'

'Yes, that's right, Heinz. How did you know?'

'Fishermen know this way to catch fish and, of course. Der wilddieb.'

'Der wilddieb, Heinz. What's that?'

'Hm.' Heinz frowned. 'Der dieb. That is a thief. Und wild...'

'You mean a thief who catches wild animals and things, Heinz?'

'Ja. That is so.'

'Someone who catches rabbits with a wire snare?'

Heinz nodded. 'Ja. A wild animal thief.'

Tim was about to laugh but stopped himself. He hated it when someone laughed when he was trying to speak German. Mr. Morgan always did that, but Tim didn't think it was because he wasn't doing well at German. He was. In fact he was much better at speaking it than most of his class, even though they'd been in Germany much longer than he had.

'We call that kind of thief a poacher, Heinz.'

'A poacher. Ah.' Heinz tried the word again. 'Poacher. Gut.' He nodded. 'Good. Gut. Aber I was telling you how to catch this fish, ja?'

'Sorry, Heinz. How do you do it?'

Heinz smiled. 'You… How you say kitzeln?' He let go of the steering wheel with his right hand and twiddled his fingers back and forth near his ribs, laughing.

'Tickle,' said Tim. 'Do you mean tickle? When you make someone laugh?'

Heinz nodded. 'Ja. Tickle. Kitzeln.' He continued to twiddle his fingers. 'If you know where fish like to rest near the bank you can do this very carefully.' He lowered his hand slowly and wiggled his fingers, curving them in slightly. 'Und so…' He smiled. 'You tickle the water by this fish. He like the feel… Und dann…' He curved the fingers more tightly. 'You move the hand fast, und…' He jerked his arm up.

'Have you done this?' asked Tim.

'Na, ja.' Heinz nodded. 'When I am a boy, Mr. Tim.'

'Were you a poacher, Heinz. Ein wilddieb?'

Heinz laughed. It was a deep throaty laugh. Tim liked it. It was a bit like old Mr. Runciman's laugh, only louder.

'Nein, I am not a poacher.'

Tim was about to ask how you could tell where the fish liked to rest when he saw movement ahead. 'Slow down, Heinz! Careful. There's an old man coming out of the ruins onto the road.'

'Ja. I have seen him.' Heinz was changing gears.

As Heinz slowed right down there was the roar of a powerful engine to the left of the Volkswagen. A large, gleaming wet black shape drew alongside sending a thick sheet of muddy water over the smaller car. Then it surged forward. It was the black Mercedes belonging to Mr. Welch. It sped past and then swerved sharply to the right in front of the Volkswagen. Heinz jammed on the brakes and the Volkswagen skidded to a stop, but as it did so Tim saw the Mercedes swerve again, this time into a huge puddle at the side of the road, close to the old man who threw up his arms to shield his face as muddy, gritty water, thrown high by the wheels of the speeding black car, covered him from head to foot. The Mercedes sped on as the man, arms flailing wildly, fell to the ground. He struggled up slowly, filthy water dripping from his clothes. He reached down for a battered old hat. Then, looking fearfully towards the Volkswagen, he ran back into the ruins, clambered over several piles of rubble, and disappeared.

'Schwachkopf! Idiot! Schweinhund!'

Tim had never heard Heinz get mad. It was obvious from the word 'idiot' that he was calling the driver a fool, maybe something much worse, maybe something rude. Heinz was shaking his fist at the fast receding car as he shouted each word.

'Schweinhund!' he thundered again. Then he looked at Tim, his face red and angry. 'One day I tell you about that coward.' He jammed the car into gear and the car jumped forward. 'Schweinhund!'

There was silence in the car for the rest of the journey to Hohenzollernring School. Tim had asked Heinz to check on the old man, but Heinz wouldn't do that. He said he had strict instructions from Tim's father to look after Tim while Dad was in England and he wasn't leaving him in the car or taking him into the ruins.

Chapter 15

DOUBLE SUMMER TIME

At school, during the morning break, Tim heard Reggie Welch laughing. 'My dad's driver let's me steer the car sometimes. You should have been there this morning. I soaked some old Kraut good and proper.' He turned and saw Tim. 'Huh! There's the fraternizer. His stinky old Volkswagen slowed down to let the old geezer cross the road.' He laughed. 'But I showed him!'

An older boy, walking past the crowd gathered by the steps, turned and stopped. He was a prefect. His name was Smith and he was captain of the cricket team. 'It's not his Volkswagen that stinks, Welch, it's your car. It smells of fish.'

'Hey! What…?' Welch turned and then saw who it was. He hesitated, and then stuck out his lower lip aggressively. The lip had healed but there was a small scar and another beneath the lip. 'We've got the best car in the district. My dad's an equivalent major. He's in Supplies and Distribution and he's…'

'So what!' said Smith. 'My father's an equivalent major too. Our car doesn't stink. Being an equivalent major has nothing to do with it.'

'I didn't mean that,' said Welch. He looked round. 'What I meant was, some people have it given them on a plate; not my dad. He's had to climb, to work his way up.' He looked round again. 'He's made it.'

'So what!' said the prefect. He shook his head. 'You must have a really big chip on your shoulder, Welch.' He shrugged. 'Anyway, your car stinks. You might not notice it but I can smell it a mile off. And it's not the smell of that sewer you live next to, either.'

Some of the boys standing nearby started to snigger.

Reggie Welch glared at them 'Shut up!' he said, fingering the scar below his lower lip. 'Just shut up!'

'No, you shut up, Welch,' said Smith. He turned and walked away, some of the crowd following.

Welch stared after him, his face red. His grey-blue eyes narrowed as he turned towards Tim. He opened his mouth to say something but the ringing of the bell cut him short.

Tim smiled. At least there was someone at the school who told Welch off. He could feel Welch staring at him as he walked up the stone steps into the entrance hall. All the way up the stairs he could sense Welch behind him. Dad was right; Welch was trouble. But he didn't have to put up with Welch kicking his chair anymore; Welch had been moved to a seat on the far-left side of the classroom. Things weren't so bad after all. If only... he thought of Dad, wondering how he was getting on in England.

*   *   *

It was baby Jane's birthday. The party had gone well. Mum had made a special cake and Sarah and Tim had helped her ice it in the kitchen. Then they took turns scraping the bowl and licking the icing off their spoons. Inge was giving Jane a bath and getting her dressed.

In pink icing sugar across the top Mum wrote: *Jane's Special Double Daylight-Saving Cake – 1944 – 1947*. She had difficulty getting the date on.

'Why have you written that, Mum?' asked Sarah.

'Because we chose Jane's birthday, dear.'

Tim nodded. 'Don't you remember, Sarah?'

Sarah shook her head. She looked down at her feet. 'No,' she said simply.

'I remember,' said Tim. 'It was because of Hitler.'

'Hitler?' said Sarah. 'What do you mean?'

'Now you've really confused Sarah, Tim,' said Mum. 'You must remember that Sarah wasn't as old as you. And there were flying bombs coming down all over the place. Sometimes it's difficult to remember anything but those dreadful doodlebugs with their tails of flame.'

'I remember those,' said Sarah. 'And Tim helping me with my gas mask.'

'Tim nodded and breathed in deeply. He'd never forget the gas mask, or the doodlebugs; the dreadful staccato roar of the rocket engines, that harsh, grating, menacing sound before the silence as the engine cut out and the flying bomb fell. He found himself counting as he had done in those days: *one and two and three and…* He shook his head and felt tears in his eyes as he remembered his friend, John, killed when a bomb hit the old pub, the Rose and Crown where John was staying with his grandparents.

'Are you all right, Tim?'

Tim took a deep breath. He nodded. 'Yes, Mum.'

'But how did we choose Jane's birthday, Mum? And what about Hitler?' Sarah frowned. 'I can't remember. How did we do it?'

Tim remembered the day when baby Jane was born at the nursing home in Crowborough.

'We decided not to let Hitler win,' said Mum. 'Jane arrived just seconds after midnight, that is to say midnight of Double Summer Time.'

'But,' said Tim, 'the doctor said we could choose to make it before midnight or after midnight, whatever we wanted, as he said it was only because of Hitler, because of the war, that we had Double Summer Time and not just ordinary Daylight-Saving Time.'

Sarah shook her head. 'I don't understand.'

Mum smiled. 'It's difficult, Sarah, but on ordinary time Jane's birthday was on Sunday; on Double Summer Time, which was only introduced because of the war, it would have been on Monday. So we chose Sunday.' She sighed. 'Poor old Dad wasn't home then and he isn't here today; and as Double Summer Time finishes early this Sunday morning Dad will miss out on Jane's special cake.'

'But we can save some,' said Sarah. 'Dad can have it when he gets back next week.'

'It's not quite the same,' said Tim. 'I know what Mum means. It's not like having it on the day, the last birthday Jane will have in Double Summer Time.'

'I hear what you are saying about Jane's cake,' said Heinz, later. 'And I hear what you say about the rocket bombs, Mr. Tim. They were bad, nicht wahr? Did they destroy your house?'

Tim shook his head. He was in the basement cleaning his shoes for school; Bits was sitting at his side. He scratched the Boxer's head.

'Our house was destroyed by a bomb,' said Tim, 'at the beginning of 1940. That was when I almost died, Heinz.'

'I remember. You told me about the mask for gas.'

'And that was when Bits died, Dad's dog.'

The Boxer barked.

'Not you, Bits, you silly old thing.' Tim spat on the cloth wrapped round his right forefinger and rubbed it in the tin of black polish. His shoes were beginning to shine, beginning to get that 'spit-and-polished' look like army boots.

'So that is why the Major is in England, about your house?'

'That's right,' said Tim. He nodded. 'But then we got bombed out of another house.'

'Two houses, Mr. Tim. I did not know that.'

'It wasn't our house, Heinz. It was one Dad rented in the country, so we'd be safe.' Tim shrugged. 'But we still got bombed. It was near John's place, my friend who was killed by the doodlebug.'

Heinz nodded and remained silent.

'Anyway,' said Tim, 'you were going to tell me about the coward.'

Heinz looked puzzled.

'You know, Heinz. Mr. Welch's driver.'

'Ah. Ja.' Heinz pursed his lips and breathed out slowly through his nose. He nodded. 'This is a secret, ja?'

Tim nodded.'

'Hans Zeiger: that is his name. It is because he is a coward that he hates me.'

'I don't understand, Heinz.'

Heinz sighed, looking down at the floor. He reached over and fondled Bits' ears. 'It was the desert, in North Africa.'

'But I thought you were an engineer, Heinz, not in the tank corps.'

Heinz nodded. 'You are right, Mr. Tim. I am not in the Panzers, I am an engineer, but I am a specialist in mines. That is why I help Major Athelstan, your father.'

'Oh! I see. So what happened?'

'This Zeiger; I saw him let another soldier die.' Heinz clenched his fist. 'He thought I was dead also. I was lying in the sand for two days. It felt like two years.'

'You mean you were in the blazing sun for two days?'

'It is not sun all the time.' Heinz closed his eyes, breathing deeply. 'At night it is very cold. I was nearly dead when they find me.'

'Who? Who found you, Heinz?'

'The soldiers who came to bury the dead,' said Heinz, simply.

'The coward!' said Tim, angrily. 'Zeiger's a rotten coward!'

Heinz nodded. 'He is. Aber, there is more. He claimed an act of bravery that I know another man did.' He shook his head. 'I could not prove it. I was in field hospital three months and didn't see him for over a year. He had been given a medal and had been promoted.'

'That's rotten,' said Tim. He thought about Dad and Mr. Welch. Dad had been badly wounded, and if it hadn't been for Sergeant Morse Dad might be dead. But Sergeant Morse hadn't been promoted like Mr. Welch. Maybe Mr. Welch wasn't a coward like Zeiger, he probably wasn't, but it was something like the same thing. And now this coward, Zeiger, worked for Mr. Welch. It was strange the way things happened sometimes.

Heinz was shaking his head. 'When I saw him again I am very angry, for now he is officer like me. I tell him what I know and he just laughs; he knew I could not prove it.' Heinz looked up. 'Then I hit him.' He smiled. 'It felt good but it was idiot thing. I was demoted from officer.' He nodded slowly. 'Now I am driver.'

'But so is Zeiger, Heinz.'

'Ja. I know. Und I often wonder why.' He shrugged. 'Aber, this is our secret. Ja?'

'Ja, Heinz.' Tim smiled and Bits licked his hand for attention. 'When are you going to teach me more dog commands, Heinz?'

The driver smiled. 'Tomorrow, Mr. Tim, tomorrow.' He looked at Bits. 'I have asked at many houses near here like the Major asked me. No one knows this dog. No one ask for this dog. He is lucky to be alive.'

'I know,' said Tim. 'The vet said he would have died lying there in the field.'

'Ah. Das ist wahr. He would have died. But what I mean is he has not been eaten.'

Tim looked at Heinz. Had he heard what he thought? 'Did you say eaten, Heinz?'

'Na, ja! Do you see many animals, Mr. Tim?'

Tim thought about this. It was true. Apart from Bits he could remember seeing only two other dogs: one belonged to Mrs. Beecher; it was a dachshund, a sausage dog; Mum said she treated it like a baby; the other was a very large Alsatian at the Royal Engineers' depot in Hamburg; it was a guard dog; Bits was wearing one of its collars.

'Do you mean that people eat dogs, Heinz?'

'People eat anything if they have hunger.'

Tim was thinking about this as he took Bits for a walk after supper. The Boxer walked quite well now, able to put weight on his right leg with only a slight limp. The vet had removed the cast but Bits had a splint for support. This was the third evening they'd gone out together and Bits found lots of places to stop at and sniff.

Tim hadn't been paying much attention, simply enjoying the quiet of the evening, when he realized where they were. Without knowing it he'd turned onto Schulhaus Strasse. They were close to the crater. In the dying heat of the day the smell from the crater was very strong. To his left was the orchard; the apples were beginning to form and fill out and Tim wondered if the drought would affect them.

Bits had his head raised, snubby snout in the air, his nose twitching. He growled quietly, deep in his throat. Something had attracted his attention. Tim looked towards the Welch house. Zeiger, the driver, was walking down the driveway; his right hand gripped the metal handle of a steaming bucket, his left hand held a mop. He walked to the rear of the shiny black Mercedes and opened the boot. Then he rolled up his sleeves, dipped the mop in the bucket and brought it out dripping with soapy water, steam rising on the evening air. He started to scrub the inside of the luggage space.

Chapter 16

PEACE IN OUR TIME

'Very thoughtful of him,' said Dad, cutting a piece of meat pie and lifting it to his mouth. It was steak pie, made from stewed, tinned steak from Denmark. It was one of Dad's favourites. Mum had made the pie as a special treat for Dad's return from England.

Tim knew Dad was being sarcastic. His voice had that edge to it.

'Well, at least the new people won't have to move into the house at Pooh Corner,' said Mum. 'I think it's rather decent of Welch.'

'Decent! He's never done a decent thing in his life,' said Dad. 'Not that man. There has to be a reason. There has to be something in it for him.'

'Well, I must admit their house is lovely, Will, the best in the neighborhood. I can quite see why he would want to keep it.'

'Huh!' Dad shook his head. 'That's true. It's a better house than Colonel Farnmore's. How Welch managed to wangle that I'll never know.'

'Don't always be so suspicious, Will. Mrs. Farnmore told me her husband chose their house because of the garden. The Colonel loves gardening.' Mum smiled. 'Like you.'

'True,' said Dad grudgingly. 'Maybe I do misjudge Welch sometimes.' He shook his head. 'I just can't help it. The sight of him makes me mad.'

'Well, in a week or so he and his family won't be around for a while so you don't have to worry about that,' said Mum. 'Muriel Welch was telling me that the sewer repairs will start soon, so they're taking their holidays early to avoid all the noise and the dirt.'

'Huh! There you are then.' Dad shook his head. 'As I thought; there's nothing decent about Welch not moving! It didn't take long for our Supplies and Distribution expert to arrange that, did it! The temporary drain channel was only put in two weeks ago; it was plenty good enough for now, with all the other reconstruction work that needs doing.'

'I don't know anything about that,' said Mum. 'All know is that it smells and with this hot weather it's worse than ever. Muriel Welch says it's unbearable.'

Tim was thinking furiously since Mum mentioned the upcoming sewer repairs. He was calculating his pocket money over the next few weeks; there was no way he could save enough Baffs to buy the camera to take pictures before the sewer was repaired.

'So, you are still talking to that woman,' said Dad.

'If you mean Muriel Welch, yes I am.' Mum looked up, her blue eyes flashing. 'As I said before, Will, I hear she has a terrible time with that man. Terrible! There's no need for her whole life to be a misery. Audrey Beecher agrees with me.'

'Hm.'

Tim took a deep breath. 'Dad, can I ask you something?'

'You're mother's talking, Tim.'

'I've finished, Will,' said Mum. She turned to Tim. 'What is it, dear?'

Tim looked from his mother to his father. 'I want to buy something at the NAAFI, Dad.'

'Buy something from the NAAFI?' Dad chuckled, shaking his head. 'Now how on earth did we get from talking about the Welch family to you wanting to buy something at the NAAFI? We're going there tomorrow, anyway.'

'That's just it, Dad.' Tim sighed. How was he going to explain?

'Well, come on, Tim. Out with it!'

'It's that camera I've seen. It's not expensive but I don't have enough Baafs to get it yet.'

'Then you'll just have to wait, dear,' said Mum. 'You know what we've always said: If you have to save for something, to wait for it, you will enjoy it all the more.'

Tim nodded. 'I know that, Mum, but I want to make a record of us being here in Germany and if I have to wait then Pooh Corner will be gone.'

'Ah. I see.' Dad nodded, his lips pressed together, moustache bristling. 'Perhaps we can work something out.'

On the drive home from the NAAFI in Hamburg Tim couldn't stop examining the camera. He couldn't believe it was his. He wouldn't have any pocket money for another six weeks, but it was worth it. He couldn't read the instructions for the camera as they weren't in English; but while they'd had tea at the Carlisle Club, after shopping, he'd studied the diagrams. He'd load the camera when they got home. He had to be careful though not to get any light on the film; there were only eight exposures. Dad said they would use the shelter as the darkroom and he'd look into getting the chemicals needed to develop the film; he'd done that as a boy. He seemed quite excited. Then he'd mentioned something about a sunlight frame and contact paper to make prints.

The Opal began to bounce and sway as Dad pulled onto the unmade road. Sarah and Jane were laughing, pretending to bounce and sway more than was necessary. Tim smiled and looked out of the window. They were passing the ruins by the river, the ruins he could see through the binoculars in the attic at Gustav Strasse Sieben. He held the camera close to the window and tried to peer into the rectangular viewing glass. It was no good, the swaying of the car and the awkward angle made it impossible to keep the image steady.

He was turning away when the car passed an open area, a short stub of cleared road in the rubble. Walking slowly, side by side, were the German boy and the old man Reggie Welch had drenched with water. Some of that water would be good to have now for the gardens and fields. The boy seemed to be leading the old man, holding his hand.

'Look!'

'What is it, Tim?' Mum turned towards him.

What was he going to say? If he mentioned the boy and what had happened Dad would think he was a fraternizer. If he mentioned the old man and Reggie Welch, and Zeiger letting Welch steer, he would just get angry and might even give away Heinz' secret.

'Nothing, Mum.' He looked down, pretending to examine the lens of the camera. 'I'm just not used to all these ruins yet.' Now he's lied to Mum. He felt his face getting hot.

'Hm.'

Tim looked up. Mum was frowning, staring at him, one eye covered by a lock of curly brown hair. She opened her mouth, about to say something.

'By the way,' said Dad. 'Something I forgot to mention when I got home yesterday. The drought has really hit the potato harvest in England. It's hard to believe. The war has been over for two years now but the food situation seems to be getting worse.'

'It's the same here,' said Mum. 'Apart from that downpour while you were away, Will, it's been hot and dry. Just look at the potato field behind the house! Goodness knows what kind of crop that will yield.'

Tim breathed a sigh of relief. Dad had changed the subject just in time. Mum was good at asking questions; questions that somehow made you talk.

It was a week since Dad had returned. No one had mentioned the escape of the SS officer but, on the wireless the British Forces Network radio news was full of the trials taking place in Hamburg, and especially the trial of the Stalag Luft lll Gestapo officers. Tim could tell that the thought of the SS officer being free was never far from Dad's mind. And the papers were full of reports from the military courts and Dad loved to read the papers after dinner, although Mum tried to hide the section with reports on the trials before he got home.'

Tim liked reading the paper, too, and whenever he got the chance he'd read the reports on the trials.

MURDER ON THE AUTOBAHN
-----*-----
HANDCUFFED OFFICERS

Hamburg, July 7.-

The court heard today a description of the murder of Squadron Leader R.J. Bushell, of Cape Province, and Pilot Officer B.W.M. Scheidhauer of the Free French Air Force, on the Autobahn near Saarbrucken. The description was contained in a statement by Gestapo officer, Emil Schultz. The two Allied pilots were handcuffed behind their backs and...

Tim read a few more lines but then had to stop. The report was becoming very descriptive and he felt sick. But he was puzzled. That Free French officer had a very German sounding name.

'What are you reading, Tim?' Mum was seated in a large wing-backed armchair in an alcove by the bay window in the living room. The alcove overlooked the back garden and was her favourite spot. Outside the window was a peach tree and, although other crops might not be doing well, it looked as if there would be a bumper crop of peaches. Baby Jane was tucked in beside Mum. Mum was showing her words in The Radiant Way, the same book Mum had used when she had taught Tim to read. Sarah was in the kitchen with Inge, making pastry.

'I was reading about the relics of the Saxon raiders they've found in Kent, the relics of Saxons who landed in England hundreds of years ago. Then I was reading a report about the Stalag Luft III war crimes trial, Mum.' Tim turned as he heard the sound of the Volkswagen enter the driveway.

'Hm. I thought I'd hidden that part of the paper.' Mum looked annoyed. 'Quick! Put it under a cushion, Tim.' Mum pointed to the sofa.

But before Tim could fold the paper the door opened and Dad walked in. He was shaking his head.

'I heard that, Enid. I know what you're trying to do, arranging dinner while the news is on, hiding the paper. There's more in the paper than news of the trials. I hear all that at the Garrison office, anyway,' Dad sighed. 'I know I get annoyed and I'm bound to be upset, but it doesn't help to hide the paper; and you know how much I enjoy an after dinner read.'

'I'm sorry, Will.' Mum handed baby Jane the Radiant Way book and stood up.

'I'm reading, Daddy.' Jane held up the book, her blue eyes shining. 'Look.' She waved the book back and forth.

Tim knew Jane couldn't really read, not yet, but it was jolly good that she wanted to.

Mum smiled. 'I'll make tea.' She laid a hand on Dad's arm as she passed.

'Just what I need.' Dad smiled. 'And talking of newspapers, while I was in England I read about a new play by that Noel Coward fellow.'

'I love musicals,' said Mum, turning.

'It's not a musical, Enid. It's a play. It's called Peace in our Times. Coward has set it in an England taken over by the Nazis. Can you imagine if that had really happened?' Dad rubbed his fingertips together. 'Jack-booted Gestapo and SS officers strutting around London. Hitler in Buckingham Palace!'

'Hitler in Buckingham Palace!' Tim almost jumped up from the table. 'What would have happened to the King and Queen?'

'I don't know, Tim.' Dad shook his head. 'Perhaps Hitler would have set up the Duke of Windsor as a puppet king. The Duke and Mrs. Simpson knew Hitler. Always visiting Germany before the war began.'

Tim hadn't known that. He couldn't believe it. The man who had been King Edward VIII for a few, short months, a friend of Hitler! He was glad he'd abdicated and married that American woman. 'Anyway,' said Dad, 'enough of that. Let's have tea and talk about the summer holiday. I'm marked down for leave at the end of August, the last two weeks. I thought we'd go north, to the seaside. There's a nice hotel on the Isle of Sylt. Terrific place! Lots of sand! Wonderful swimming! I'm told that the water's so clear you can see your feet even when standing in deep water.'

It sounds wonderful,' said Mum as she opened the door to the kitchen. 'You'll love that, Tim, won't you?'

Tim nodded glumly and put the newspaper on the table.

Part 2

THE BOY

Chapter 17

A RICKETY OLD BICYCLE

'Now that you've been at the school for a while, Tim, I think you can take the bus home in the afternoon instead of Heinz having to drive out of Hamburg to pick you up.'

'That's fine, Dad.' Tim nodded. All the other boys rode home in the bus, including Welch. That would be the only thing: Reggie Welch. Tim took a bite of his cucumber sandwich. Reggie was driven to school and back by Zeiger but caught the bus home on Wednesday. Why was that? It was odd!

'The bus stop is just up the road, Tim' said Mum. 'I'll meet you with Bito. In fact I'll bet that after the first few days that old dog will know when you're coming home and go to meet the bus on his own. Where is he by the way?'

'He's sitting by Tim's feet.' Sarah lifted the tablecloth and pointed.

'You're not giving him food are you, Tim?'

Tim shook his head. 'No, Mum.' He reached down and scratched Bit's head. Bit's stubby tail thumped on the floor.

Tim took another bite of the cucumber sandwich and thought about the bus. He wouldn't mind taking the bus; in fact he was pleased. Now, maybe, he could find out why Reggie Welch took the bus home on Wednesdays. And he would find out just in time; the Welch family was going on holiday at the end of this week before school closed for the summer; and Reggie, lucky as usual, would miss the end of term exams.

Wednesday came at last and Tim climbed onto the bus. Reggie had got on first and taken a seat at the front on the right. He hadn't noticed Tim waiting in the crowd. Tim was with a noisy group. He turned his head away from Reggie and pushed his way down the aisle to a seat on the left side, a seat by the window. The two children in the seat in front were small, and by peering over the top of the seat he could see Reggie.

Twenty minutes later the bus approached Altona station. Tim could see the DP camp to his right, the curved metal roofs of the Nissan huts shining in the sun. Tim wondered which hut was the one Mr. Kotsko lived in.

The bus slowed down. It didn't stop at the station itself but about a hundred yards beyond, away from the crowds gathered at the station entrance trading black market goods. Reggie stood up. Tim knew that some of the children got off here, but what was Reggie doing? He hadn't been talking to anyone who got off here, keeping himself to himself. But as the bus slowed to a stop, Tim saw Zeiger a little way off, standing next to the black Mercedes. So that was it. There was no mystery at all. For some reason Zeiger met Reggie here and took him home. Tim felt disappointed.

The bus driver pulled a lever to open the front door and got off. He lit a cigarette and watched as the Altona crowd left the bus. Reggie followed. Some of the children were met by drivers, some by women who were obviously maids, and some by their mothers.

But Reggie was moving away from the crowd, towards the station, not towards Zeiger. What was he doing? A scruffy man pushed his way out from the crowd and walked quickly towards Reggie. Reggie stopped and nodded. The two disappeared into a doorway at the side of the station.

Tim got up from his seat and hurried down the aisle, keeping his eye on the doorway. The bus driver had his back to the bus enjoying his cigarette. Tim went down the two metal steps, careful not to tread too heavily and make a sound that would attract attention. He walked on tiptoe along the side of the bus and round the back. Now the driver could not see him if he turned round. There was the doorway where Reggie had disappeared. Tim ran, his satchel bouncing against his side with every step. He reached the side of the station and glanced hurriedly behind him. No one seemed to have noticed. He inched his way carefully along the grey stone wall to the doorway and peered round the edge of the opening. Reggie and the man were not there but he could hear muffled voices.

Tim crept slowly into the opening. It was dim inside, out of the sunlight and he stopped to let his eyes adjust to the semi-darkness. There was a short passageway and then a junction with another passage to the right and one to the left. He could hear the voices much better now, but there was an echo and he couldn't be sure in which direction they were coming from. He moved slowly down to the left. Reggie was saying:

'Next week I want more pens. I'll trade you one chocolate bar for two pens.'

'Ja, ja,' said a deep voice. 'Das ist gut. I bring more pens.'

Tim couldn't believe his ears. Reggie was trading on the black market. And at school he traded one pen for two chocolate bars! That meant that for every pen he made a profit of three chocolate bars. No wonder he was podgy and fat!

'I have to go now,' said Reggie.

'Ja,' said the man. 'Aber, I need cigarettes too.'

'I'll see what I can get,' said Reggie. 'Dad might not miss a few. I'll trade you ten pens for one cigarette.'

There was a throaty laugh. 'Ten! Ha! I trade five.'

'Eight,' said Reggie. 'Eight for each cigarette.'

There was a pause. 'Sieben. I give seven pens.'

Tim could almost imagine Reggie nodding his head. 'Okay. Seven. Make sure it's seven.'

Tim had now oriented himself to the direction of the sound. Hurried footsteps came towards him from the passage on the right. Tim shrank back against the stone wall and hoped he was hidden from view. His heart was pounding. But he need not have worried. Reggie was in such a hurry that he ran down the passageway and turned to the entrance without glancing in Tim's direction.

But what was the scruffy man doing? There wasn't a sound. All was quiet. Tim had to get out of here and back to the bus. He crept back down the passage to the junction. There was a scraping sound and then the flare of a match. The scruffy man was lighting a cigarette. Tim could see him clearly in the bright yellow light of the match his head bent slightly forward, his hands cupped round the flame. He was only a few feet away.

Tim hesitated for a split second and then ran towards the doorway brilliantly lit by sunlight. There was a shout behind him and the pounding of large, heavy feet. He was almost at the doorway when he felt a hand snatching at his jacket. He shook it off and ran with all his might, through the doorway into the sunlight, towards the bus, straining with the effort, his lungs feeling as if they would burst. He saw Welch getting into his father's car, closing the door. The Mercedes drew away and headed towards the road.

Tim raced for the bus but the driver didn't see him! He was closing the door! The bus moved off! Tim wanted to shout but he knew that if he did he would only attract the attention of the black market crowd, not the driver. The bus had now reached the road and was gathering speed. The man behind him was laughing, a weird, tinny laugh

Tim kept running. The bus was disappearing in the distance, but if he got to the road then he might be able to stop a car, stop an army vehicle, anything! Someone would stop when they saw him in his school uniform, wouldn't they? Then he saw a rickety old bike, bent and rusty in places, but he recognized it.

'Hey! Mr. Kotsko! Help!'

The man on the bicycle slowed and glanced behind him.

'Mr. Kotsko! Mr. Kotsko!' Tim waved.

The bicycle came to a juddering halt. The pounding footsteps behind Tim slowed and then stopped.

'Mr. Tim! What are you doing here? This is dangerous place, not a safe place for someone like you.'

Tim nodded. He glanced behind him and saw the scruffy man disappearing into the black market crowd. 'I'll explain later. But I have to get home or Mum will worry when I'm not on the bus and I'll be in big trouble.'

'Trouble is not good. I'll get you home, Mr. Tim. Sit on the crossbar and hold on tight. I go by a track and I can beat that bus, it makes so many stops.'

Tim eased himself onto the round metal crossbar and gripped the handlebars as Kotsko pedaled away from the station. The bicycle made funny clattering noises as it gathered speed. The gardener turned left onto a rutted dirt track and pedaled furiously. Tim felt every bump, every dip in the track as the bicycle bounced up and down. But he didn't care; soon he'd be home safe and sound; and he'd never go to the station again.

Chapter 18

SWIMMING LESSONS

The summer holiday had begun and Reggie Welch was away for a month. How Mr. Welch had managed to wangle a month off, when everyone else got two weeks, was something Dad couldn't understand, but he said the CCG man was such a wheeler-dealer, such a scrounger, that nothing surprised him anymore.

Tim didn't care how long the Welch family was away. He wouldn't have to worry when passing the house at Pooh Corner when he went to the Country Club, not for a while at least; there would be no Mr. Welch to glare at him. But Tim did see Zeiger at the house and, for some reason he couldn't explain, he hurried past when the driver was there even though Zeiger didn't take much notice of him; he seemed to be more interested in the repairs to the sewer than anything else.

Another thing about the holiday was that he did not have to face Mr. Morgan at school. And in September he'd have a new teacher. The only good thing he remembered from Mr. Morgan's class was learning why the Free French pilot murdered at Stalag Luft lll had a German-sounding name. It had come up in a geography lesson. Geography seemed to be Mr. Morgan's favourite subject.

'Some of you may have been following the war crimes trials taking place here in Hamburg.' Mr. Morgan looked round the class. No one said a word. 'And you may have wondered how a French pilot had a name that sounds more German than French.' Mr. Morgan carefully smoothed a few strands of straggly dark brown hair across his scalp to the right side of his bald head. He peered at the class through his thick lenses. 'Can anyone tell me his name?'

Tim put up his hand but the teacher ignored him and continued to look round the room.

'I know his name, sir.' Tim waited, but still the teacher didn't look in his direction. 'Schneidhauer,' said Tim. 'Schneidhauer, sir!'

From his new desk on the far left of the room Welch looked round at Tim and smiled. 'It's Schneidhauer, sir. His name's Schneidhauer.'

'Right, Welch. Well done.' Mr. Morgan smiled and looked at Tim. 'Well done, Welch,' he said pointedly. He stepped up to the blackboard. 'Now here I've drawn a map of Europe. Here, to the left is France. Here, to the right, is Germany. Just above France is Belgium and down here we have Switzerland.' He looked round and then turned the chalk sideways. 'Here is Alsace Lorraine.' He drew the chalk across to the right and then down the board in a thick upside down L shape. The chalk screeched. Tim shivered. 'There! A piece of land between France and Germany! First one country has owned Alsace-Lorraine and then the other, and so on and so on. As a result, some people have French names and others German. It's valuable territory, on the river Rhine. It's full of coal and iron and France and Germany have fought over it for hundreds of years. For the past two hundred years most people living there have spoken French even though many have German names. When the war began it was part of France.'

So that was why.

One day, early in the school holiday, Tim was on his way to the Country Club. Over his right shoulder he carried a home-made fishing net. In his left hand was a large glass jar swinging from a thick string handle he'd tied round the neck. He'd practiced swimming in the pool most days in the past two weeks, but not when Sarah and Jane were there. He still couldn't swim properly. When his sisters were at the pool he went to the fish ponds, but he hadn't seen the boy again.

Tim's feet crunched on the gravel path between the rhododendrons. He crossed over onto the grass verge. That was better. Soon he was crossing the large stretch of open grass leading to the first pond. He thought about the article he'd read in the newspaper about Saxon relics being dug up in Kent: knives, swords, shields and buckles. It was odd to think that perhaps, fourteen hundred years ago his ancestors may have been among the Saxon raiders from Germany who landed in England and could have walked on the ground he trod on now; maybe that's why he recognized lots of German words.

There was no one at the first pond; nobody ever seemed to be down here, except the German boy. Tim nodded. Maybe the boy had Saxon ancestors too. He shrugged.

The rhododendron bushes hid the ponds from view from the Country Club buildings; and the path, if you didn't follow it through the long grass, seemed to lead nowhere especially now that it was so overgrown. Tim was pleased, it made the place more secret, his secret. The tiny fish darted back and forth just beneath the surface of the pond. They seemed to be a little bigger than they were when he first came to the pond. Tim left the jar and his net on the grass and visited the other ponds, but there was no sign of the boy. He returned to the first pond and picked up his net; it was made from a cotton McDougall's flour bag, a metal hoop made from a wire coat hanger, and a length of thick bamboo that Mr. Kotsko had given him. The net was similar to one Grandpa George had made when Tim and Sarah stayed at Corvuston in 1944. The fine cloth of the bag was ideal as water drained out, but not too quickly so that the catch could be scooped up into the glass jar.

Tim wanted to catch some small fish. There was a pond in the back garden of Gustav Strasse Sieben, not a natural pond but one built of brick like the house. The pond was about eight feet long and five feet wide, like a small swimming pool, shallow at one end, deep at the other. But the deep end wasn't really deep as it was only about one-foot-six inches deep. Mr. Kotsko said that was why there were no fish in it; it was so shallow that the local herons could easily reach the fish. Dad had stretched chicken wire over the top, not to keep herons out but to keep Bits out.

Now that he was better, Bits romped round the garden and had jumped in the pond to cool off. The July sun was scorching and sometimes Bits had lowered himself into the waters until only his eyes and nose were visible. When he came out he was not only wet but muddy too. That was when he usually ran up onto the paved verandah and shook himself, splattering the French doors with water and flecks of mud. At one point Mum got so mad she threatened that Bits had to go. Dad came home with the chicken wire.

Tim smiled. Maybe he should bring Bits with him to the ponds one day; Bits would like the ponds. Tim undid the buttons of his shirt; it really was hot.

Before he started to fish he decided to dip his feet in the water. He took off his rubber-soled plimsolls and placed them next to the jar; the white canvas uppers of the shoes were reflected in the glass, gleaming from the chalky-white Blanco he'd used to clean them. He sat on the grassy bank and slowly lowered his feet into the cool water of the pond. The water lapped gently at the bank turning a light yellow-grey where movement disturbed a thick bed of clay.

It was so refreshing that he sat there idly twiddling his toes his eyes half-closed. A shoal of small fish swam round his feet then darted away as if one. Tim felt for his net and gripped the sturdy pole. He leaned forward looking for more fish. There! Gently he lowered the net into the water, under the fish and pulled it up quickly. At least six! Water ran slowly out of the bag. Tim got up and poured the fish into the glass jar. He was right. Six! They were all silvery-grey, flashing in the sun as they darted back and forth. Tim smiled as he put the jar in the shelter of a large rock.

He sat back down on the bank and waited. The fish seemed to know why he was there and swam just out of reach. He leaned out further, but as he did so the bank crumbled and he almost fell in headfirst. The thick bamboo pole saved him, but when he pulled it out the wire hoop was draped with weed, badly bent and muddy from being pressed on the bottom. But he hadn't fallen in! He was standing in water up to his waist.

Tim had an idea. Stripping off his shirt he threw it onto the grass. Rinsing the net he slowly edged into the pond, feeling the depth with the end of the pole. The pond wasn't deep and in the centre the water barely reached his armpits, so he wasn't out of his depth. Tiny fish brushed against his legs, tickling, and the mud on the bottom of the pond oozed between his toes. The water was warm. He tried a few swimming strokes but had to put his left foot down, almost bouncing along on his big toe, head held high out of the water. He'd bring Bits next time. He could hold onto Bits and they'd swim together, and he wouldn't have to worry about anyone seeing him learning to swim.

He stood up and threw the net like a javelin onto the grass. It landed beside his shirt. He waded towards the bank. As he did so a small figure darted out of the bushes and raced towards him. It was the boy. But as the boy neared the pond Tim realized he wasn't running towards him but towards his clothes.

'No! Nein! Nein!' Tim shouted. 'Leave my things alone!' He pushed himself through the water, trying to get to shore. Then his feet slipped from under him.

Tim felt his head go under and the water close round him. He thrashed his arms and legs in panic; he couldn't breathe! It felt like a terrible weight was pressing down on his back and a vision of the air raid shelter at Hampstead swam before his eyes. His reared up out of the water and screamed. The German boy was staring at him, blue eyes wide with fear. Water poured into Tim's mouth and he gagged, sinking back beneath the water. He couldn't breathe! It felt as if the clammy rubber of a gas mask was pressing into his face. But he wasn't wearing a gas mask! He was in a pond! He thrashed again and again.

Then he felt hands tearing at his hair, pulling at the roots. He was moving through the water. He still couldn't breathe but as he reached up he felt grass and mud beneath his hands. He dug his fingers into the thick clay at the edge of the pond and, straining with all his might pulled himself forward. He felt warm, damp grass beneath his chest. He could breathe! The hands were no longer gripping his hair.

Tim gulped in a lungful of hot, dry afternoon air and opened his eyes. In front of him were two wet, sandal-clad feet. The straw soles of the sandals were sodden and the strips of cloth that bound them to the small feet were stained with clay, mud and grass. He started to look up when his stomach heaved uncontrollably. Dirty water poured out of his mouth. The feet moved sharply back.

'Bist du gesund?'

Tim took a deep breath and looked up. The German boy was staring down at him. His blue eyes seemed huge in his thin face.

'You saved me.' Tim's throat hurt and he could hardly speak.

'Bist du gesund?' repeated the boy.

Tim took another breath. He knew that bist du meant are you; the boy was asking if he was all right. He felt like crying he'd been so scared. He nodded. 'Ich bin gesund,' he said haltingly. 'Danke.' He hoped that was right.

'Das ist gut.' There was a brief smile on the boy's lips; then he bent down and grabbed Tim's shirt in one hand and the net in the other.

'Hey!' Tim tried to shout then felt his stomach heave again. When he looked up the boy was running in his strange awkward way towards the bushes. Tim struggled to his feet. 'Hey! Come here!'

The boy looked back and waved. Tim's shirt was like a white flag in his hand.

Tim shrugged. What could he do? He felt ill. He couldn't chase the boy. And what was he going to tell Mum? He waved back and the boy was gone.

'What do you mean, someone stole it?'

'It's true, Mum.' Tim had showered at the Country Club pool and cleaned up before walking home. He was feeling a lot better.

'Why would anyone at the club steal your shirt?'

'I don't know, Mum.'

'They probably needed one,' said Sarah.

Mum glared at Tim. 'Clothes are hard enough to come by without you losing them, Tim.'

'I know, Mum. Sorry.'

'Well, use a locker next time, instead of leaving your clothes lying around for anyone to find. I'm not at all happy about this.'

'Yes, Mum. Shall I feed Bits?'

'Oh, dear. It's in one ear and out the other. Have you been listening, Tim? You can feed that animal later.'

'I was listening, honest I was, Mum. I didn't want anyone to steal my shirt.' Tim didn't know if that was a lie. When he'd thought about the boy running off with his shirt he'd felt pleased in a funny sort of way. It was a kind of way to say thank you for helping him.

'Well, I don't know where I'm going to get another one. You only had two that fitted you; now you're down to one. Oh, dear.' Mum shook her head and fiddled with the keys on her belt. 'I'll talk to Mrs. Beecher. She has a seamstress who makes her clothes. I've no idea where she gets the material, but I'll ask.'

Tim waited.

'Well, I suppose you have to feed that dog.' Mum sighed. 'Here you are.' She held out a bowl full of scraps. 'I do believe that animal eats better than many people I see around here.'

'Like people in the ruins, Mum?' asked Sarah.

Chapter 19

THE NIGHTMARE

Tim awoke drenched in perspiration. He was struggling for breath. Why was his light on?

'What is it, Tim?' Mum stood by the bed, her hand on his forehead. 'Hm. You're not running a temperature. But I heard you cry out and when I came in you were mumbling something about a mask. You haven't had that nightmare again, have you?'

Tim struggled to sit up. He felt weak and had a pounding headache. 'I was dreaming about the shelter, Mum.' Tim's throat was dry and it was difficult to talk. 'When I was buried in the shelter when our house was bombed.'

Mum shook her head, a worried frown on her face. 'The shelter? Whatever brought that on? You haven't had that nightmare for years.' She pushed the fair hair back from Tim's forehead, out of his eyes. 'You were mumbling something about a fraternizer and then something about drowning.'

Tim breathed in deeply. What else had he been saying? He really had felt he might drown in the pond, until the German boy pulled him out. He shuddered. It was good to be awake, to have Mum in the room. The nightmare had started differently this time:

He was racing across a field. There was someone behind him, breathing down his neck, tearing at his shirt. Somehow he knew it was Reggie Welch, but he wanted to be sure. He looked back and tripped. He started to fall down, down, down into clear cool water; he knew it was water because of the bubbles rising up in front of the visor of the gas mask. The gas mask! Why was he wearing the mask? He couldn't breathe! There were fish all around, small fish, large ones. They kept bumping into him, brushing past, hitting the filter on the mask. Their tails moved back and forth, slowly at first, then faster and faster, stirring up mud, creating a swirling, muddy mist. It was impossible to see! He hit out in all directions fighting to swim upwards; then finally he surfaced. Reggie Welch was there with Mr. Morgan.

'He's a fraternizer,' said Welch, pointing an accusing finger at Tim.

'I knew it.' Mr. Morgan nodded. 'I knew he was a troublemaker.'

'Tim! Tim!' Mum was shaking him. 'What is the matter? Are you sick?'

Tim stared at Mum and a terrible thought crossed his mind. Suppose the water in the pond was contaminated? He'd swallowed quite a lot! Suppose he was sick; not like at boarding school, but really sick! But that couldn't be. Mum said he didn't have a temperature. And there hadn't been any bombs round the Country Club; Dad had said that Alstermarschen was one of the few places close to Hamburg that hadn't been damaged.

'Tim! Talk to me! Is something worrying you?'

What could he say? If he told Mum what had really happened, the boy would be in trouble for stealing. The police would look for him. He'd saved Tim from drowning; that would help him, but he was not only trespassing at the Country Club, he was poaching, stealing fish from the ponds, maybe selling them on the black market?

'Tim. There's something wrong, isn't there?' Mum stroked his forehead. 'Tell me.'

Tim took a deep breath. He'd have to tell. 'It's all because I can't swim, Mum, and I thought I would drown.'

'Can't swim?' Mum frowned. 'What on earth are you talking about? And what has swimming to do with gas masks?'

'I really can't swim, Mum, and now I'm afraid of drowning, not being able to breathe, like I felt in the gas mask during the war.' Tim looked down at his hands; he was gripping his right hand with his left.

'What do you mean you can't swim? Of course you can. I saw you swimming in the sea at Eastbourne last summer.'

Tim sighed. 'I had one foot on the bottom, Mum. I was pretending.'

'Pretending?' Mum shook her head, her blue eyes puzzled. 'But you've been going to the pool each day.'

'I know, Mum. But I can't swim. I can't and I'm scared I'll drown. I'll never swim.'

Mum smiled. 'That's silly, Tim.' She ruffled his hair. 'Fancy worrying yourself sick, dreaming about a thing like that. You should have told me you couldn't swim.' Mum yawned. 'I'll talk to Mrs. Beecher.'

'But…'

'No, Tim.' Mum yawned again. 'I'm too tired to talk about swimming at this unearthly hour. Now, no more talking! Stop worrying and get some sleep. Come on, I'll tuck you in.'

A week later, as Tim climbed the stairs to the attic he was smiling. Mrs. Beecher was a really good teacher and, although he was terrified at first at being in water again, she had persisted, gently persuading. And! No one else was around for his lessons. Good old Mum!

'Think of something else, Tim,' Mrs. Beecher had said as she cupped her hand under his chin. 'Swimming is a little like flying, so just relax and remember what I told you.'

It was when Mrs. Beecher mentioned flying that it happened. It was like the time during the war when he overcame the fear of wearing a gas mask. He'd imagined he was a pilot flying a Lancaster bomber and putting on an oxygen mask so he could breathe.

'L-for-Lucky Lancaster,' he whispered.

'What was that, Tim?' asked Mrs. Beecher.

'I was thinking of something else, Mrs. Beecher, like you told me.'

'Good! Now remember I've got you. Push out!'

'L-for-Lucky Lancaster,' he whispered. 'L-for-Lucky Lancaster. L-for Lucky Lancaster.'

'Well done, Tim!' Mrs. Beecher was standing about ten feet away! 'See! You swam those last strokes without my help.'

Two days later he was swimming in the deep end, diving in from the springboard. He still didn't like the feel of water closing over his head but his arms and legs thrust him to the surface each time and he swam strongly to the side, ready to dive in again.

'Super, Tim!' Mrs. Beecher smiled. 'You don't need me anymore.'

'Thanks, Mrs. Beecher.' Tim wiped his face on the towel and pushed his hair back. 'Thanks a lot. But I would like to learn to swim on my back.'

'Fine, Tim, I'll talk to your mother.'

When he'd dried off and changed, as he had done for the past two days, Tim went down to the ponds. He wanted to see if the German boy was there. Since the nightmare, when Mum had stopped him talking, he hadn't found a chance to tell her about the boy; or was it that he really didn't want to say anything?

He walked carefully on the grass verge beside the gravel path, pausing as he neared the end of the rhododendron hedge. The long uncut grass was beginning to turn yellow and brown in patches. Dad said the drought was becoming a major problem. When would it rain?

Tim hurried across the open stretch, the long grass brushing against his bare legs. The sun beat down warming his back. There was no sign of the boy at the first pond. Tim found the gap in the hedge and inched his way through to the far side. The boy wasn't at the second pond either. He ran round the pond to the far side, to the next hedge. As he neared the hedge he heard a strange sound on the far side, a sort of popping noise. He stopped and then slowly and quietly edged forward. What was happening at the third pond? He eased his way into the thick foliage and peered through.

There were two men on the far side of the pond. One of them was Zeiger. What was he doing here? The other man was tall and thin and was slowly emerging from the bushes on the far side, looking carefully about him as he did so; he hadn't seen Zeiger yet and it was obvious that Zeiger hadn't seen or heard him either. The thin man was holding a stick in his right hand and was gently tapping it against his leg. Zeiger stooped and reached into a large hessian sack on the ground by his feet; as he did so the thin man stopped and then quickly stepped behind a tree. Zeiger straightened up and with a sweep of his left arm threw something out into the water. Hundreds of tiny splashes erupted over the surface. Tim nodded; that was the sound he'd heard.

Zeiger bent and reached into the sack again. He was feeding the fish. Why? What did he have to do with the ponds? As Zeiger threw the food out over the water the second man crept furtively back to the bushes, seeming to melt into them. He was hiding. Tim frowned. Had he seen this man before? He shivered. For some reason he couldn't explain he felt scared. Slowly, carefully, avoiding stepping on any dry twigs, Tim moved back from his hiding place in the bushes and ran.

Tim reached the top of the stairs. Dad was out for a walk with Bits; he said he wanted to be alone for a while. Occasionally Dad came home really happy, but most days he was quiet, brooding. He didn't get angry so much any more, but sometimes it was better not to try to talk to him. It was at those times that Bits seemed to understand; he would sit quietly waiting by Dad's chair, his ears pricked up head on one side. Then they'd go for a walk.

Tim could hear music coming from Inge's room. She had a small wireless that Dad had given her; it wasn't the best radio and crackled and whistled a lot, but it worked. The crackling and whistling reminded Tim of his crystal set. He'd left the crystal radio at Grandpa George's house at Corvuston. He wished now that he'd brought it with him.

He pushed open the door to the furnished room. The sun was setting and a rosy glow lit the grimy windows and shone on the bookshelves. He must look at those books one day. He kept forgetting to do that.

The binoculars were pointed towards the ruins as he'd left them. He stepped up onto the box he'd found to replace the footstool and swung the binoculars first to the right and then left. Could he find it? Yes! There it was: a short stub of cleared road in the rubble. All was quiet. Nothing moved.

Then, coming into view from the right were two figures: one was bent and old, the other was short and had close-cropped dark hair; he wore a white shirt that was too big for him, and slung across his back was an old cloth bag. It was the boy! He held the old man's hand, leading the old man to the far end of the road. There they climbed a low mound of bricks and then seemed to slowly disappear into the ground.

Tim waited to see if the boy would re-emerge, but all remained still. Then, slowly, a thin wisp of silvery-white smoke rose out of the ruins, turning pink in the final rays of the setting sun.

Chapter 20

TWO SCRUMPERS

'These are junge Karpfen, Mr. Tim.'

'Young what, Heinz?' Tim stared into the garden pond at the six small silver-grey fish. They waited just below the surface. They wanted food.

'I don't know the name in English,' said Heinz. 'In German we say Karpfen.' He pronounced the name slowly.

'Carp! Carp!' said Tim. 'I've heard of them. That's what they are. Young carp.'

'Carp,' said Heinz, smiling. 'Karpfen. It is the same, ja.'

'Well, almost,' said Tim. He nodded. 'Karpfen.'

'They grow big.' Heinz held his hands about a foot apart. 'Two years this size. Three years,' he stretched his hands out to about eighteen inches. 'They eat much food.'

Tim nodded. 'What do I feed them, Heinz?'

'They eat anything, Mr. Tim. I show you.' Heinz turned over a sandy-coloured flat rock. Ants scurried across the ground, along tiny winding trails that disappeared down holes in the ground. 'Ameisen,' said Heinz, pointing. He picked up a short, thick twig and stirred it around and around in the centre of the uncovered ground, boring downwards. Soon hundreds of soft, white ant eggs littered the ground. Heinz scooped some up and threw them into the pond, brushing ants from his hand.

The fish shot to the surface and gobbled up the eggs. Tim was busy digging for more eggs. He wasn't having much luck. Ants poured out of the ground up the stick and onto his hand. He threw the stick on the ground. 'Will they eat bread, Heinz?'

'I think so, Mr. Tim. Aber, one day I remember mein Grossvater und meine Grossmutter taking me to a… I'm not sure in English… ein Mönchs-Kloster.' Heinz shook his head, obviously thinking. 'Mönchskloster,' he repeated.

'Monks,' said Tim softly. 'Cloister. Is that what you mean, Heinz, a monk's cloister, a monastery where there are lots of monks?'

'Ja! Ja!' Heinz laughed. 'Das ist gut, Herr Tim.' He chuckled. 'You learn German quickly.'

Tim smiled. 'It's just that if you listen, a lot of words are similar. A lot aren't, of course.' He nodded. 'Anyway, what happened at the Mönchs-kloster?'

'Ah! Ja!' Heinz rinsed his hands in the pond. 'At the monastery there are ponds. The monks keep fish for food and I watch them feed them. They have big sacks of food made into small…pille.' He held the forefinger and thumb of his left hand slightly apart.

'Like a pill,' said Tim. 'A pellet.'

'Ja!' Heinz smiled. 'Eine pille. Ein kügelchen, a pellet?'

Tim nodded. So that's what Zeiger was doing. Tim was about to ask Heinz if he knew anything about the ponds at the Country Club when Mum called.

'Time for your lesson, Tim! Don't keep Mrs. Beecher waiting!'

'I've got to go, Heinz. Mrs. Beecher's teaching me the backstroke this morning. I can do the breaststroke, the crawl and the sidestroke. I like the sidestroke best.'

Tim dawdled as he walked back from the club, enjoying the shade from the trees at the top of Schulhaus Strasse. But as he neared the crater the smell of the sewer grew stronger and he quickened his pace to get past. It was always the same: it wasn't so bad in the early morning, but by afternoon the hot summer sun had made the stench almost unbearable. The repairs were proceeding fast and soon the crater would be closed in. But in the meantime it stank! How could anyone work all day in the heat and with that stink? As he came near the Welch house Tim saw Zeiger leaning on a barricade, pointing, laughing at something. He must be so used to the smell that it didn't bother him anymore. When he saw Tim he scowled.

Tim shrugged and walked past. Maybe Zeiger hadn't noticed the smell in the Mercedes because of the smell from the sewer. Maybe that's why Welch hadn't noticed.

He came to the cemetery. The tombstones that weren't broken were upright again. Ahead was the orchard. It was a little like the orchard outside Medbury, on the road to Tunbridge Wells. There was a grassy bank just like Medbury, but here, with the drought, the grass was dry, straw-coloured and brittle. On top of the bank was a fence, or what had once been a fence. The wire between the posts was gone in most places and what was left was rusty and broken.

Tim remembered the day two years ago when he was riding his bike past the orchard at home. The apples looked really inviting. It had been a hot day like today and he stopped to rest, leaning his bike against the bank. And before he knew it he was in the orchard gathering apples, stuffing them inside the front of his shirt. As he scrambled back down the bank he felt a large hand on his shoulder.

'Hello, hello. And what do we have here?' It was Mr. Howard the village policeman. 'Been scrumping, have we? Well, well, well.'

Tim shook his head, remembering the way Mr. Howard made him sit down and eat all the apples he'd taken. It was awful! They weren't as ripe as they'd looked from the road. He'd had a terrible stomach-ache and he couldn't tell Mum or Dad or he'd have been in worse trouble. He went to bed that night feeling very, very sick.

He looked up at the orchard. There were some ripe-looking apples just by the fence. His mouth was dry. Perhaps there were some windfalls. Taking a windfall off the ground wasn't really scrumping, was it?

Tim scrambled up the bank. The dry grass made it difficult as it was slippery. When he reached the top he paused and looked back. Zeiger was gone and there was no one in sight. He was in luck. There on the ground was a large apple with rich red skin. He picked it up and turned it over; it was rotten. White grubs wriggled in the bright light of day. Some dropped to the ground. Tim wondered if the fish would eat them. He dropped the apple. There was another. He picked it up and brushed it off. Perfect!

Tim put his towel and swimsuit on the ground and sat down, his back against a tree. Ever since he was three, when he'd been stung by a wasp as he sat on the grass in the garden at Hampstead, he was extremely careful. He could almost feel that sting now. It was quiet in the orchard and the heady smell of ripening fruit almost overpowered the smell from the sewer. It was hot. He leaned forward and took off his shirt. As he bit into the apple, cool sweet juice ran over his tongue. He closed his eyes and was about to take another bite when he heard someone running, and then a deep angry voice shouting.

'Halt! Halt! Dieb!'

Racing through the trees, wearing his old tattered shirt was the German boy. His arms were pumping up and down as he strained to outdistance the huge man who was chasing him. His deep blue eyes were wide with fear and his lips were pulled back taut against his teeth. He saw Tim and hesitated. The man had stopped shouting and was gaining ground.

Tim darted out from the shelter of the tree and headed for the bank. The boy was right behind him. They slid down the bank side by side, but when they reached the bottom the German boy was breathing heavily. He sank down, head in his hands. Now that he was close Tim thought the boy was probably a year younger than he was.

'Nein! Nein!' Tim grabbed the boy's hand and pulled him to his feet. 'Come!' He pulled the boy behind him as he started to run.

'Halt!' The huge man was running along the top of the bank, but that was a mistake; as they came to Klein Flottbeker Weg the fence was in much better repair. As the man looked for a way to climb the fence Tim dragged the boy across the road and turned into Gustav Strasse.

Behind them Tim heard the pounding of heavy feet on the pavement. The man had found a way out. Tim's mind was racing. If they went to the house the man would know where he lived and they'd be caught anyway. They were nearing Mrs. Beecher's house. She hadn't dawdled on the way home from the Country Club; there she was in the garden, at the side of the house weeding in the shade. Her Dachshund lay nearby sleeping in the sun. The front door of the house was open. Tim made a decision. He gripped the boy's hand more tightly, flung open the Beecher's gate and raced up the garden path. They were at the door.

'Halt! Halt! Dieb!' the man shouted.

The Dachshund was now awake, barking shrilly. Glancing over his shoulder Tim saw Mrs. Beecher turn towards the road. Tim slammed the front door shut as the man turned into the garden shaking his fist, his face red and blotched with anger and the strain of running.

'Come!' Tim dragged the boy through the hall to the living room. He could hear the scrabbling of tiny paws at the door behind him. On the far side of the room the French doors were open. They raced into the garden.

Tim could hear Mrs. Beecher shouting. 'Help! Police! Someone help me!' Her voice was shrill and the dog was yapping in accompaniment. Now someone was banging on the front door. It spurred Tim on. He dragged the boy down the garden and made for the fence to his left.

'Come on! Climb over!' He pushed the boy forward. 'Climb over!'

Now they were in the Marchant's garden; they were on holiday; so were the Briggs next door. Thank goodness!

Two more fences and they were in the back garden of Gustav Strasse Sieben. Tim stopped to catch his breath, his heart pounding. There was shouting at the front of the house; that was why they had seen no one; everyone was in their front gardens seeing what all the commotion was about. Bits was barking excitedly.

'Whatever is going on?' Mum's voice was very loud and very clear. 'Mr. Kotsko! Mr. Kotsko! Please come with me, and bring the dog, there's something awful happening at the Beecher's house.'

Tim waited until he heard feet running down the road. Bits was barking louder than ever. The German boy was crouched on the ground whimpering. Tim grabbed his shoulder. 'Come on!' he said. 'Come on!' What was the matter with this boy? He pulled him to his feet and dragged him, stumbling to the back of the house. The basement door was open. The house was quiet.

'In here.' Tim pushed the boy into the basement towards the shelter. 'You hide in there,' he said, pointing.

The boy looked at him, tears in his eyes. 'Danke.' He looked exhausted, skin stretched tightly over his cheeks, dark shadows under his eyes.

Tim nodded and pushed him into the shelter. 'Stay there! I'll be back later.' He closed the door and locked it, slipping the key into his pocket. He couldn't risk anyone finding the boy now.

Chapter 21

ONE HUGE COMMOTION

Jumbled thoughts rushed through Tim's head as he raced down the path through the back garden. The German boy was safe, locked in the shelter. But Tim had to get his towel and shirt and swimsuit. If he lost those there'd be trouble. Mum would be furious after the loss of the other shirt. And, oh boy! If the farmer found his clothes he'd give them to the police and they'd trace them back to him.

He pushed through the beech hedge and turned right, running along the edge of the potato field. There was another field to cross before he came to Klein Flottbeker Weg. As he passed the Beecher's he could hear raised voices. One was the farmer's. Good! He was still there. Tim ran on, avoiding passing near the old farmhouse, through the next hedge and into the field beyond. No one! Good! The cabbages were pale and yellow and the ground was dry and powdery. He ran on.

When he reached Klein Flottbeker Weg he was exhausted. He'd run all the way home, dragging the boy with him, and now across the rough, dusty fields. He was out of breath. He still hadn't fully recovered from being ill at boarding school. But he had to go on!

There was Schulhaus Strasse. He looked up and down the road. No one! He climbed over a gate and ran on, scrambling up the bank into the orchard. Which tree was it? Ah! There it was, the white of the towel standing out like a signal flag. And there was his new shirt. In the centre lay a rich red apple.

As he strolled up Gustav Strasse, pretending he was taking his time getting home from the club Tim began to worry. He should have left the apple behind. Suppose, just suppose the man recognized him; he'd better get rid of the apple But it was too late, baby Jane had seen him.

'Tim! Come and see!'

Inge turned. Baby Jane was perched on her shoulders holding tightly to Inge's short dark curls. She waved. Then Bits came bounding out of the crowd, his tongue lolling and his stubby tail wagging round and round with excitement. He pushed his flat, damp, slobbery snout into Tim's hand.

'This is an outrage!' Tim heard his mother's raised voice. 'An absolute outrage!'

Then Tim saw Zeiger. He was standing at the back of the crowd looking at Tim, a puzzled expression on his face.

'Come and see what's going on, Tim.' Sarah was pushing her way through the crowd. 'Come and see!'

It was no use. Mum had seen him now. Two red spots always appeared on her cheeks when she was angry; today they were huge. She looked down at Tim's feet and frowned. What was Mum looking at? Tim looked down; his plimsolls which had been white early this morning were now a dusty yellow-brown, so were his legs, dust from the dry earth of the cabbage field up to his knees.

A military policeman was by the gate talking to Mrs. Beecher. There was a German policeman taking notes in a small black book.

'The point is this,' said Mrs. Beecher. 'I don't have any children; not one and certainly not two boys.'

'Yes, ma'am, I've got that.' The army policeman removed his peaked red-banded khaki cap and scratched his head. His hair was very short; short back and sides Dad would call it. 'But do you know any youngsters, anyone who might visit?'

'Of course I know lots of children.' Mrs. Beecher laughed. 'I'm a teacher. And I give swimming lessons too. But I can't say that children visit me. And they certainly wouldn't charge through my house as these two evidently did.' She looked round. 'Now there's a boy I know.'

Tim felt his heart skip a beat as Mrs. Beecher pointed to him. The military policeman looked at Tim, so did the German policeman and the farmer.

'You haven't been visiting today, Tim, now have you?' Mrs. Beecher smiled. 'Of course you haven't.'

The farmer was shaking his head, looking away.

Tim breathed in slowly and carefully. He didn't want to look as if he was relieved. He shrugged. 'What's happening, Mum?'

'I'll tell you later, Tim. For someone who's been swimming you look as if you've been dragged through a hedge backwards. Get yourself home and tidy up before lunch. I won't have you at the table like that.'

Tim wasn't going to let this opportunity go. He pushed through the crowd and hurried down the street. Bits trotted along beside him. As he neared the house Tim had a strange feeling; he shivered and looked back over his shoulder. Zeiger was turning away, hurriedly. Had the driver been watching him? Had he seen the apple?

Tim hurried round the back of the house into the basement. Bits followed, his nose in the air, sniffing, making short, sharp, high-pitched whimpering noises.

'What's the matter, Bits?' Then Tim realized. Bits could smell the boy. That was it! Bits knew the boy! They must have been together that morning in the field when Bits was beaten. Things were getting worse! Now Bits was snuffling at the door of the shelter. Tim put his towel on the workbench. The apple rolled out. Thank goodness it hadn't fallen out at Mrs. Beecher's. He'd give it to the boy, but he must be quick, everyone would be home soon. If it wasn't for Bits the boy could stay in the shelter till dark. But now he had to get away.

Tim took the key from his pocket and unlocked the door. Bits pushed past, sniffing and whining, turning this way and that. The shelter looked empty! Where was he hiding? Tim was looking under the bunk bed on the left when he saw Bits pawing at the door to the garden. It was then that he saw the door was ajar and the padlock hung open on the hasp. Open!

Tim scrambled to his feet. What was going on? He lifted the lock from the hasp very carefully and looked at the numbers: 7843. Was that the combination? Was it just chance, or did the boy know the numbers somehow? Bits was scratching at the base of the door. It swung open and Bits charged out round the side of the house.

'Bits! Bits!'

Bits was gone! Tim knew it in his heart. He wanted to cry. His shoulders drooped. Poor old Dad. He loved Bits. Tim shook his head. What had he done? He closed the door and put the lock through the hasp and shut it. He spun the dial.

7-8-4-3. Tim set the numbers carefully one by one. As number three clicked into place the lock opened. He shut it and did it again. He didn't think it was luck; the boy knew the combination! Was this his house? Was that why he was standing nearby when Tim had arrived from England?

As he locked the padlock for the second time Tim's heart skipped a beat. Bits came charging back through the basement door from the back garden. He was barking excitedly. There was the scrabbling of paws on the wooden stairs and as Tim came out of the shelter he saw Bits disappear through the door to the kitchen. Was the boy upstairs? Was he still in the house? Oh, no!

Tim ran up the stairs. The kitchen was empty. Now Bits was running up the main stairs. Tim followed. Bits came charging out of Tim's bedroom, knocking him over. Tim scrambled to his feet laughing; as he did so Bits tried to run up the stairs to the attic but they were so steep he had to slow down.

'What are you doing, Bits?'

Tim followed, holding on tightly to the banister rail; he didn't want to be knocked downstairs backwards if Bits came charging down. He could hear the dog pacing round and round, sniffing. When he reached the small landing Bits was in the old furnished room sniffing at the bookcase by the window.

The glass front of the bookcase was open at the middle shelf and there were books on the floor. Tim looked at them in surprise; he hadn't bothered to look at them yet, thinking they'd all be in German, but now he could see they were books he'd read himself. There was *Treasure Island,* the cover a dark blue with a picture of a sailing ship imprinted on the cover in gold leaf. And here was a copy of *The Settlers in Canada.* They were very like the books Grandpa George had at Corvuston, books Dad had read as a boy. Tim opened the cover of Treasure Island. In purple ink was printed: WERNER KIEBEL. The letters were obviously made with a rubber stamp set. Tim opened another book. This one was written in German but had the same name stamped in purple ink inside the cover.

Tim looked round the room. Who was Werner Kiebel? Was he the owner of this house? Then he noticed something else wrong in the room. At first he couldn't place it but then realized what it was; some of the pictures were off the wall. There was one on the desk, face down; the wire was missing. He checked the others that were down. All were missing the wire to hang them up!

Tim's mind flashed back to the morning they'd found Bits in the potato field; he'd been tripped by a snare! The boy was the poacher; he caught rabbits and he'd taken the wire from the pictures to make more snares. That was it! But how had he known, and why come up here?

'Tim! Tim! Where are you?' Mum was calling.

'Up here, Mum! I'm up here in the attic!'

'What on earth are you doing up there? I thought I told you to get cleaned up before lunch. And what's this dog doing up here?'

Mum was on the landing at the foot of the attic stairs. Bits was halfway down, finding it difficult to descend the steep narrow staircase.

'I think someone has been in the house, Mum, while you were at Mrs. Beecher's. Bits came tearing up here and I followed him. There are pictures off the walls.'

'Pictures off the walls? What do you mean? What on earth is going on?' Mum started up the stairs.

'Watch out, Mum!'

It was too late. Bits was three stairs from the bottom when he jumped, knocking Mum over. Then he bounded down the lower stairs.

Tim ran down and helped Mum. She got slowly to her feet, looking dazed. 'Are you all right, Mum?'

Mum nodded slowly. 'I think so, Tim.' She rubbed her right elbow. 'This has been an amazing day so far. And now we'll have to check everything in the house to see what's been stolen.' Her right hand felt for the keys on her belt. 'I hope we don't have any more surprises. Now get yourself cleaned up. Lunch in ten minutes.'

Chapter 22

PEEPING TIM

The rhythmic beat of the Opal's tires, speeding over the joints in the concrete-paved road reminded Tim of the clickety-clack of train wheels on iron rails. The wide concrete Autobahn stretched straight ahead for miles and miles. Tim knew that distance was measured in kilometers in Germany but he still couldn't help thinking in miles.

At last they were setting out on holiday.

'I'm glad Colonel Farnor spoke to the Brigadier,' said Dad, 'or we might be on our way to the Isle of Sylt instead of Travemunde.'

'It must have been awful,' said Mum. 'Imagine not being able to swim at the seaside and in this heat too. I must admit I am a little disappointed at not going to the officer's hotel; I'm told it's beautiful.'

Tim was disappointed too, not because of the hotel but because he'd been looking forward to driving across the causeway to the island; you could only do that at low tide because at other times the sea covered the narrow strip of road connecting the island to the mainland. One of Sarah's friends had been to Sylt and said it was fun driving along the narrow road with the sea on either side. And she'd told Sarah that the sandy beaches were super.

'I agree,' said Dad. 'I can't imagine being at the seaside and not being able to go in the sea.'

Tim breathed a quiet sigh of relief. At least he no longer had to worry about swimming as he was quite good at it now, but he still had a fear of being out of his depth for any length of time. He'd stay close to the shore so he could put his foot down if he wanted to feel the comfort of solid ground.

Dad was shaking his head. 'The Colonel said there were jellyfish everywhere. One woman almost died when she dived in. She'd only just arrived and was so hot that she didn't notice that no one else was in the water. She was stung on her face, arms and neck.'

'Agh! Horrible!' said Mum. 'I'd rather not talk about it if you don't mind.' She wound the window down a little further. 'It's not too drafty for you in the back, is it?'

'No, Mum,' said Sarah. 'It's lovely.'

'Inge? What about you?' Mum turned round, her curly brown hair blowing in the wind.

'It is gut, Frau Athelstan. And the baby Jane is asleep now.'

Tim looked at his little sister; she was curled up on Inge's lap, her right thumb in her mouth. With Jane on Inge's lap there was plenty of room, but if Bits hadn't run off and he'd been with them it would have been crowded. 'I bet Bits would have loved this ride,' he said sadly.

'Yes.' Dad nodded. 'He couldn't have come with us to the Isle of Sylt, but you say the place we are going to doesn't mind dogs, Inge.'

'Ja, mein herr. They take families with dogs.'

'Well.' Dad sighed. 'It would have been fun to have Bits along, but I don't expect we'll see that old dog again.' He shook his head. 'It really is extraordinary. That morning when we found Bits injured, he must have been with one of those boys the farmer from the orchard was chasing two weeks ago. The farmer was probably the one who beat the dog.'

Tim looked out of the window. The car was speeding past open country but he didn't really see it; he was thinking about the German boy. Every day the situation seemed to get more complicated. At first it had been a relatively small thing: not helping Reggie Welch catch the boy and Welch calling him a fraternizer; Mum and Dad still didn't know about that. Now he was a real fraternizer, actually helping the boy escape by hiding him in the house. And there was still the matter of the combination lock and the picture wire for rabbit snares. He shook his head. At some point he knew he would have to tell.

'It wasn't the farmer, Dad.' Tim shook his head. 'Not the one at Mrs. Beecher's house; he was big and heavy. The man who beat Bits was thin.' He shivered.

'I see.' Dad nodded, watching the road ahead. 'Well then, the man who beat Bits must be the farmer who owns the potato field.'

As Dad talked Tim called to mind the scene on the morning they'd found Bits: there was the silhouette of the tall thin man against the early dawn sky; he was slapping his leg with a stick. And yes! Now Tim thought about it, wasn't the man watching Zeiger at the pond slapping his leg with a stick? He was tall and thin! He hadn't connected the two things before but now the two scenes flashed back and forth in his mind. He shivered again; that must be why he had that scared feeling. He had to tell Dad somehow without involving the boy and getting him into trouble.

'Bitte, Herr Athelstan.' Inge was pointing. 'You go that way.' She pointed to an exit ahead. 'Lübeck. Then mein freundin is not so far and Travemunde is not so far.'

'Right.' Dad nodded. The hum of the engine became quieter and the mesmerizing rhythm of the tires ceased as Dad turned onto the exit, off the Autobahn and down the concrete ramp.

If they had gone to Sylt, Inge would have stayed at the house at Gustav Strasse, but when Mum learned that Inge had a friend near Travemunde she'd insisted that Inge come with them and have a holiday too.

On the way, Inge had told them the legend of Lübeck, the legend of the marzipan. It had happened five hundred and forty years ago, when Lübeck was under siege. There was no grain left in the city to make bread. The people were hungry. But the granaries were empty of grain and only stocked with sugar and almonds.

'A reward was offered,' said Inge, 'for the one who could make something with the almond nuts and sugar.' She smiled. 'On St. Mark's Day the winner gave the people marzipan. In Lübeck, since then, it is called the bread of St. Mark.'

Tim nodded. From now on, when he ate the marzipan on Christmas cake he'd remember that.

*   *   *

'This is so beautiful.' Mum looked round and smiled. She had said the same thing each morning for the past week. 'This is exactly what Dad needed. If we had been too near Travemunde it wouldn't be half as relaxing.' She shook her head. 'And I'm so glad we're not on the Isle of Sylt in a busy hotel.'

It was another hot summer day and the gleaming white sand of the beach in front of their cabin shimmered in the heat. There were two other cabins some way away, hidden in the pine woods; both were occupied by British officers and their wives but there were no children. It was quiet.

Tim sipped his tea. It was still too hot to take a good mouthful; condensed milk didn't cool tea quickly like ordinary milk, and it tasted different. Dad always said he took three heaping teaspoons of sugar because of the taste, but Mum just laughed and said Dad had the sweetest tooth of anyone she knew.

Dad was in the water. He was swimming at a leisurely pace on his right side, his left arm rising slowly out of the water on each stroke. Tim smiled; that was his favourite stroke too, but he swam on his left side.

Dad was much more relaxed than he had been at the start of the holiday. He didn't want to go anywhere. He was content to stay on the beach in front of the small house. He spent hours in the water and lying on the sand, or sleeping in his wicker chair with the wicker doors closed to keep off the sun. He was very brown and every time he came out of the water Mum rubbed a mixture of olive oil and malt vinegar on his back. The smell reminded Tim of fish and chips and made him feel hungry. The only parts that weren't brown were Dad's fingertips and the terrible scars on his leg. The scars weren't white anymore but stood out pinkish-red against the deeply tanned skin. Tim wasn't used to seeing Dad's wounds and at the beginning of the holiday had purposely looked away. Now he tried not to stare as he imagined the pain Dad must have gone through.

Tim sighed. The rest was doing Dad good, Mum too. On the first night he'd heard Dad mention the escape of the SS man:

'I was ready, Enid. I was prepared to give evidence. Now that swine may never be brought to justice.'

Mum's voice had been raised when she said she didn't want to hear any more about it. 'Leave it alone, Will, please! Try to forget it. If that man has disappeared from our lives for good I'll be really happy.'

'But can't you see, Enid? I may never see it concluded. I'll…'

'Please, Will.'

Dad had murmured something but Tim hadn't been able to make out what he said. He'd heard nothing since. That was good. He'd be happy too if the whole thing went away. Maybe then Dad would be his old self.

'Oh! No!' The sound of Mum's voice brought Tim's thoughts back to the present.

'What's the matter, Mum?'

Mum pointed. 'Just look how far those two have gone. I wouldn't mind if they were with you but I told them not to wander too far.'

Tim looked along the beach. Sarah and Jane were quite a long way away, walking slowly by the edge of the water. Their heads were bent, peering at the sand. Tim knew they were looking for shells. Sarah had quite a large collection. He jumped up.

'I'll get them, Mum.'

As Tim started off he pretended he was in a race, but he couldn't run fast in the fine, powdery white sand; his feet sank almost to his ankles with each step. So he made his way to the water's edge. It was easier to run here as the damp sand was quite firm. The girls were still some distance away, near a group of sand dunes that formed a small point, rising up quite high and then sloping down to the shore.

'Sarah!' Tim shouted. 'Jane! Mum wants you!' He stopped and waved as Sarah turned. But then the girls carried on walking. They probably thought he was coming to join them. But why were they now walking faster? He splashed his way along the edge of the water. This was the Baltic Sea and just to the right was the Russian Zone of Germany. He quickened his pace, sprinting.

'Sarah!' He was out of breath.

'Are you coming with us, Tim?' Jane looked up. Her light brown hair was bleached blonde from the sun. It was almost as fair as when she was born. 'Are you coming 'sploring?'

'She means exploring,' said Sarah. 'We're going to look over there.' She pointed to the sand dunes.

Tim shook his head. 'Mum sent me to fetch you.'

'But listen!' Sarah put a finger to her lips. 'Shush!'

Faintly, beyond the dunes, Tim could hear laughter. There must be a beach on the other side. He wondered what it was like.

'We're going to look.' Sarah started to walk off.

'No!' Tim ran up to her. 'Mum doesn't want you so far away.'

There was more laughter from beyond the dunes. Tim hesitated then whispered in Sarah's ear:

'We'll come and explore later, when Jane's having her nap.'

Tim tied the towel round Sarah's head like an Arab headdress. 'Bedouin girls are meant to wear veils,' he said.

'Why?' said Sarah.

'Because they're not meant to seen by men.'

'That's silly.' Sarah brushed a lock of hair from her forehead and pushed it under the towel.

Tim shrugged. 'It's a rule. But you don't have to wear one; we're only pretending.'

'Well, I think it's a daft rule.' Sarah frowned. 'It's stupid. I wouldn't wear a veil.'

Again Tim shrugged. He didn't want to get into an argument with his sister; she had that look on her face. 'Come on!' he said, 'Before Jane wakes up.' He adjusted his towel, draping it over his shoulders.

They trudged through the sand to the foot of the dunes. Tim pretended he was a Bedouin chief advancing across the desert to discover who had invaded his territory. Slowly he made his way to the top of the dune. The sand sloped down into a hollow and then rose up again.

'Come on!' Tim raced down the slope and charged up the other side, nearing the top.

'Wait! Wait for me, Tim!'

Tim glanced back. Sarah was still struggling down the side of the first dune, slipping and sliding. It was better to run down as he had. He scrambled up the last few feet. There was a small beach on the other side. It was crowded with people, laughing, some sunbathing some swimming. But Tim felt his face getting red and he dropped to the sand, out of sight. Sarah struggled up beside him.

'What's the matter, Tim?'

'Nothing!' Somehow he had to stop Sarah looking over the top. 'Let's go back.' He edged forward carefully and peered over the top of the dune again. He was right; he knew he had been; nobody had any clothes on! And there, talking to a deeply tanned woman was Inge. She had no clothes on either. He slipped back and lay there thinking.

'What's the matter? I want to see!'

'Shush!' Tim put his finger to his lips.

'Why?' Sarah wriggled forward to the edge of the dune. Her eyes widened. 'Ing...'

Tim put his hand over her mouth. 'Shush! I've got to think.' He peeped over the edge of the dune and then slithered back. 'We can't tell Mum or Dad, Sarah.'

'Why not?'

'If we do, then Mum won't want to stay here. And Mum says this place is just what Dad needs to relax.'

Sarah nodded. 'So what do we say, Tim?'

Tim thought for a moment. 'Well, we don't want to lie, so we just say that it's a long way to get here and the sand is difficult to walk in. That's true, isn't it?'

Sarah nodded.

Tim crept up to the top of the dune once more and peeped over. He edged back down. 'And then we say there's nothing worth seeing.'

'Then why are you peeping, Tim?'

Tim felt himself blushing. 'I just wanted to see if they were getting brown all over.'

Chapter 23

RETURN OF THE WANDERER

The white streak in Dad's hair contrasted against the tan of his face as he leaned forward to scratch Bits between the ears. 'I must admit,' he said, 'I'm really happy to have this old dog back again.'

Bits looked up, his tongue lolling out. He closed his eyes as Dad petted him.

Dad continued: 'I still can't understand how he got into the house. Kotsko said he wasn't inside when he left at noon.'

Tim looked at his father. How Bits had got into the house had been puzzling his parents ever since their return home yesterday. Tim knew. He was positive and he wanted to change the subject.

'He's lost a lot of weight, Dad. Look at his ribs.'

It was true. Bits had lost weight and was ravenously hungry when they'd arrived last night.

'He is thin,' said Mum. 'But I can't understand it either. How did he get into the basement?'

'He probably sneaked in while Kotsko was in the garden,' said Dad. 'Kotsko told me that after he'd fired up the boiler he spent some time weeding at the front.'

'Mm. That's possible,' said Mum.

'He was probably with those boys,' said Dad. 'One of them was seen hanging around while we were away; not the taller one without a shirt, the shorter one with the cropped hair.' Dad stroked his fair moustache with the fingers of his right hand. He was frowning. 'I'm pretty sure it must have been those two who broke in here. How they did it I don't know. Maybe they sneaked in while Kotsko was busy. Anyway, besides the lock on the larder there's no sign of any other locks being forced.'

'Well,' said Mum. 'All I can say is that I'm glad I hid my keys.' Mum's hand gripped the large bunch of keys hanging from the ring on her belt. 'At least they didn't get anything besides the food.'

'Locks wouldn't have stopped them, Enid.' Dad ran his fingers through his hair. 'If they'd wanted to steal anything else they'd have soon forced the doors. And, as I said, only the larder was broken into.'

'I suppose you're right, Will.' Mum poured more tea into Dad's cup. 'All the same, it's a nuisance about the food; I was counting on certain things to make it through the week until the next ration delivery, especially the tinned bacon and Danish sausages, and the corned beef of course.' Mum put down the large brown teapot.

'Thanks, Enid.' Dad ladled three spoons of sugar into his cup and stirred vigorously. 'What's gone is enough, even though it's not a lot. And that's another thing I find strange. Why didn't they take more?'

Tim was sitting quietly listening to Mum and Dad. Why hadn't the boy taken more? Why had he left Bits behind? Of course there weren't two boys as Mum and Dad thought; he was the other boy, the one without the shirt that the farmer had chased. Two boys could have carried more food, would have. But that didn't matter at the moment; what was puzzling Tim was the combination lock on the shelter door. Why was it undone? Mum and Dad didn't know about that. He'd discovered it when he'd heard Bits barking as they entered the house on arriving home. He'd raced down to the basement; the barking came from the shelter. When he'd opened the door the light was on. It should have been off. Dad was very strict about not wasting fuel. Bits came charging out and, after giving Tim a slobbery lick, bounded up the stairs. Tim was about to run after him when he saw the lock hanging from the hasp. It was open, the numbers 7843 lined up perfectly.

'I think he did it on purpose,' said Tim.

'Did what on purpose, dear?'

'Left Bits here, Mum.' Tim nodded. 'I think the boy brought Bits here on purpose.'

'Which boy, Tim?'

'The one who was seen round here while we were away. I bet he left Bits on purpose.'

'But why would he do that?'

'Because of food,' said Tim. 'If it was me, and if I knew Bits was starving, and I knew I couldn't feed him and someone else would, then that's what I'd do.'

'Tim's right, Mum.' Sarah nodded. 'I'd do that. I'd want Bits to be fed.'

'Me too,' said Jane.

'Well from now on,' said Dad, 'keep a good lookout for those two ragamuffins. I'd like to get hold of them, find out where they come from. There's been too much thieving going on while we've been away.'

'You mean the apples and potatoes, Will?' Mum shook her head. 'I can't see that having anything to do with those boys. They couldn't have managed that!'

'No, Enid. I know. The amount of fruit stolen would fill a large army lorry, and another would be needed to truck away the potatoes.' Dad pursed his lips. His short, bristly moustache needed trimming. Dad continued:

'No, the boys couldn't have done that, but thieves hang together; they may be part of the same gang. Mind you, I'm not taking all that those farmers told the CCG at face value.'

'What do you mean, Dad?' asked Tim.

'Well, Tim, they could be using the thefts as a cover for hiding part of their crops.' Dad slowly scratched Bits' head.

'Why would they do that, Will?'

'The black market.' Dad nodded. 'The German money is worthless; you need thousands of Reichsmarks to buy anything, a wheelbarrow full of money. Food is in really short supply. The drought has been the worst Germany has experienced in years.' He shook his head and breathed in deeply. 'It's bad enough that we have drought hitting the harvest when everyone is desperate for food, but what I really find hard to swallow is farmers who deliberately hold back part of their crop while people starve.'

'It's wicked,' said Mum. 'But I thought the Control Commission had farm inspectors to make sure that sort of thing didn't happen.'

Dad laughed. 'Huh! Inspecting when it's too late! What good is that? The inspectors plan their visits to farms during the harvest. These thefts, if they are thefts, have taken place before that.' He shrugged. 'Mind you, I think any person with average intelligence could have expected an early harvest for some crops this year.'

Mum nodded. 'It's been a hot summer, hasn't it, especially after that dreadfully cold winter.'

'Well, expect more of the same,' said Dad. 'The prediction is for another harsh winter. Food of any kind will command a high price. Black market dealers will have a field day. They'll make a killing.'

Mum sighed. 'It hardly seems possible that we sat in the Four Seasons Hotel and watched people light a bonfire on the ice in the middle of the Alster!'

'I know.' Dad nodded. 'Beautiful, wasn't it.'

'And the cars driving over from one side to the other, Mum,' said Sarah.

'Cars!' said Tim. 'Cars on the lake?'

Dad laughed. 'Now you know how cold it can get here.' He nodded. 'It was so cold and the ice so thick that it didn't melt until the middle of April, just before you came. I hope we don't have another winter like that.'

'So do I,' said Mum.

Inge came into the room with a tray. Tim looked down, staring at his plate. Ever since the holiday he'd tried to avoid Inge. He felt awkward when she came near.

'Thank you, Inge.' Mum smiled. 'Danke. You know, I think it is incredible that you were so close to us.'

Inge smiled and passed the tray round.

'Did you know all the time, Mum?' Sarah smiled at the maid.

'Know what, dear?'

'About Inge.'

'What about her, dear?'

Tim butted in, glaring at his sister. 'Of course Mum didn't know, Sarah. Nobody knew.'

He looked up. Inge was staring at him through narrowed eyes, a funny expression on her face.

Later, as Tim came out of his bedroom, Inge was on the landing tidying the linen cupboard. Tim tried to sneak back into his room but the maid gently grasped his arm.

'You saw me on the beach, Mr. Tim?'

Tim looked down and nodded. He felt his cheeks getting hot.

'Did Sarah see me too?'

Tim nodded again, keeping his head down.

'Why didn't you come to say hello?'

'What?' Tim couldn't believe his ears. 'You were naked,' he blurted. 'Everyone was undressed.'

'You think bathing in the sun in just the skin is wrong?'

'Yes.' Tim looked up. 'If Mum had known, or Dad, then we wouldn't have been able to stay there.'

'But that beach is well known for skin sunning.' Inge smiled. 'Everyone there is bathing in the skin.'

'Well I don't care,' said Tim. 'It could have ruined our holiday if we'd said we saw you naked.'

Inge shook her head. 'Why, Mr. Tim? We're all the same without clothes: German, English, French, American, Russian. We're all the same.'

There was a noise on the stairs. Oh, no! Tim spun round and then breathed a sigh of relief. It was only Sarah. She looked Inge straight in the eye. 'Did you get brown all over?' she asked.

'Why do you say that, Miss Sarah?'

'Because the second time Tim looked he said you were.'

'Shut up, Sarah!' Tim could feel his cheeks burning. 'Be quiet. You make it sound as if I peeped on purpose.'

'Well, you did, too, to see if she was brown everywhere!'

'Look, Sarah,' said Tim. 'We promised not to say anything, didn't we?'

Sarah nodded. 'So we could stay on holiday.'

'Right. Now, you do like Inge, don't you, Sarah?'

Sarah looked surprised. 'Of course I do, Tim.' She turned to Inge. 'You like me Inge, don't you?'

The German girl put her arms around Sarah. 'But of course, Miss Sarah. I like you and Tim and baby Jane. I like everyone.'

'That's just it,' said Tim. 'I still think we don't say anything, because I really think if Mum and Dad knew there'd be trouble.'

'But why, Mr. Tim?' Inge looked puzzled. 'You have a good holiday, I have a good holiday. Why is that not good?'

Tim sighed. It was difficult. 'I just know they wouldn't like it, especially Mum. We don't do that.' He shook his head. 'So I bags we forget the whole thing.'

Inge took one of Sarah's hands in hers and reached for the hand Tim was about to thrust in his pocket. She knelt down and raised her dark eyebrows. 'If we forget, then can we be friends? I am your friend, you know.' Inge's forehead was creased in a worried frown and her green eyes looked from one to the other.

Sarah put her free arm round Inge's neck and kissed her. Inge smiled, her cheeks dimpled, a dark curl falling over her forehead.

'Is that special rice cake you were making cool enough to eat, Inge?' Tim grinned. He felt really happy. He liked it at Gustav Strasse Sieben.

Part 3

THE
GRANDFATHER

Chapter 24

FERTILIZER

'Hello, Tim,' Mrs. Beecher smiled. 'Did you have a nice holiday?'

'Yes thank you, Mrs. Beecher. It was super at Travemunde. I did lots of swimming.' Tim was quite pleased with himself. Over the holiday he'd been in the water so much that he'd even dived and picked up shells from the seabed. He still didn't like water going up his nose, but he didn't mind having to hold his breath.

'That's good, Tim. Are you going up to the club?'

Tim nodded. 'Yes. I'm going to practice diving.'

Mrs. Beecher shook her head. 'Haven't you heard? The pool was closed while you were away. It's empty. There was a nasty scare about the spread of Infantile Paralysis.'

Tim knew that before they went on holiday the cinemas and theatres in Hamburg had closed and, in Lünenberg they'd cancelled dances. But it wasn't just in Germany that the terrible paralyzing illness had struck; he'd read in the paper that in England, near where they'd lived in Kent, a boy his age had died. And there were lots of cases in boarding schools. Some children would be left with arms and legs paralyzed for life! Some would never walk or run again, or even get out of bed. Mum was so pleased he was with them in Germany and not at boarding school. But she didn't know about the pool at the club.

'Is it spreading here, Mrs. Beecher.'

'No, Tim. Mind you, with the hot weather and the continued bad state of the water supply it's a wonder.' Mrs. Beecher shook her head. 'You can tell your mother not to worry. This week they reported a decline in new cases. But I expect the pool will be closed for a while yet, maybe over the winter. We can't waste water refilling it.'

'Thanks for telling me, Mrs. Beecher.'

Sarah's teacher smiled. 'Now tell me, Tim. Is that dog of yours back? Bits, isn't it?'

'Yes.' Tim nodded. 'He was in the house when we got back yesterday. He's at home with Dad, in the garden.'

'Hm! How odd!' Mrs. Beecher frowned. 'While you were away I saw a dog very like Bits with that boy that hangs around here sometimes. I think he's one of the boys that farmer chased out of the orchard.' She looked directly at Tim. 'You know, it really is odd. Since that day I've never seen two boys round here, just the one.'

Tim felt uncomfortable. He hated it when anyone talked about the day he'd gone scrumping and helped the boy escape. He had to get away. 'I've got to go, Mrs. Beecher, so I'm back in time for lunch. Bye!'

'Goodbye, Tim.' The teacher looked at him. 'Please tell your mother I'll see her in the next little while.'

Tim hurried away. Had Mrs. Beecher guessed? What was she going to see Mum about? She couldn't really have guessed, could she? He hoped Mrs. Beecher wouldn't talk to Mum about the scrumping and the farmer and the two boys. He quickened his pace. He'd see what Pooh Corner looked like now. Then he'd go to the ponds.

There were no white painted barricades on Schulhaus Strasse; the road stretched clear ahead, past the orchard, past the cemetery as if nothing had ever happened. And now Tim realized what had been missing when they got home last night: there was no smell! He knew there'd been something. He crossed the road to the cemetery side to be as far away from Reggie Welch's house as possible. But he needn't have worried. The gleaming Mercedes wasn't parked in the driveway and the house was quiet.

The Country Club was quiet too, but on the patio Mrs. Welch sat talking to another woman. There was laughter from the tennis courts where Reggie's laugh was unmistakable. Tim hurried down the gravel path, his feet making a loud crunching noise at every step. As soon as he could he stepped onto the grass verge by the rhododendron hedge. That was better.

The long, uncut grass stretched out before him, yellow and parched by the long summer drought. And the pond looked less full than usual. All was quiet. Quickly, Tim made his way to the hedge and eased his way through the gap. It was quiet at the second pond too. Moving quickly he was soon at the farther hedge and was almost through the narrow gap when he heard voices. Was that Mr. Welch? All the Welch family seemed to be here today! Tim peered through the heavy green foliage.

Two men stood on the far side of the third pond, Mr. Welch and Zeiger. Zeiger was taking handfuls of pellets from a hessian sack in a wheelbarrow, throwing them out over the water. Tim watched the water churn and bubble as fish rose to feed. On the sack, printed in red was KUNDSTDUNGER. Zeiger looked up as Mr. Welch raised his voice:

'Don't threaten me!' Mr. Welch glared at his driver.'

Zeiger nodded and smiled, reaching into the sack. 'So.' Still smiling he turned to Mr. Welch. 'They will die without more food. I do not make threats, I only tell the fact.' He scattered pellets across the water.

Mr. Welch glowered at the man beside him and rubbed the back of his right hand across his mouth. 'All right, Zeiger. I'll get enough to last till winter sets in.' He laughed. 'Then we catch them and the cold freezes them.'

'Ja.' Zeiger nodded. 'Ist gut. Easy to keep, easy to move, and no smell.'

Mr. Welch nodded. 'Come on! That's enough!' He turned, heading left towards the gate on the far side of the pond.

Zeiger followed, trundling the wheelbarrow across the parched grass. Mr. Welch left the gate swinging and, as Zeiger turned to close it, Tim saw him scowl.

Tim waited a minute and then scurried across the grass. There was no gap in this rhododendron hedge so he eased himself carefully into the thicket parting the branches and treading very carefully. He could hear voices nearby.

'Tell him I want more money. This is getting dangerous.' That was Mr. Welch.

'It is dangerous for him, too,' said Zeiger.

'Maybe, but I want a bigger share: dollars, American dollars; none of those useless Reichsmarks!'

'What about more pens, drafting equipment?'

'Tsah!' Mr. Welch shook his head. 'I've got pens and propelling pencils coming out of my ears. I'll never be able to sell that lot. And even if I did, the police would be onto it soon enough.' He shook his head. 'No! I want dollars or pounds, or small easily hidden valuables: rings, jewels, things like that.'

'I will tell him.'

Tim inched forward, slowly, carefully avoiding stepping on any dry twigs, until he could see through the heavy foliage. On the other side of this hedge was a paved yard, surrounded by sheds of different sizes. Parked by a group of greenhouses was the shiny black Mercedes.

Zeiger was pushing the wheelbarrow into a small shed when it tilted to one side, tipping the hessian sack onto the ground, spilling pellets on the pavement.

'Verdammt!' Zeiger struggled unsuccessfully to right the barrow.

'Fool!' Mr. Welch pointed to the spilled pellets. 'Why didn't you tie the damned sack? Hurry!'

Zeiger bent down, scowling, and knelt beside the barrow. He scooped pellets into the mouth of the sack. Mr. Welch stood by, watching.

'Hurry it up!' He waved his hand. 'Oh! Leave it!'

Zeiger pushed himself up and tied the mouth of the sack. With a grunt he heaved it back onto the barrow. He disappeared into the small shed. A short while later he came out brushing dust from the knees of his uniform.

Mr. Welch closed the door. He took a padlock from his coat pocket. 'And remember, tell him I want to meet him; I never have yet. We can meet in the sewer.' He clicked the padlock to. 'It's the perfect place now that we have that access from the basement of my house.'

'He will not meet there. You know that. I've told you that.'

'Ha!' Mr. Welch sneered. 'Afraid of the dark, is he? Doesn't like the smell?'

Zeiger stared at the squat, pale, fair-haired man beside him. 'Nein!' He said quietly. 'He's afraid of a trap.'

Chapter 25
KUNDSTDÜNGER

On the way home Tim thought about what he'd seen and heard. Mr. Welch was up to something. Dad was right. Mr. Welch was a wheeler-dealer. Tim hadn't been able to get into the shed after the black Mercedes had driven off, but he'd looked in the side window. There were eight sacks stacked along the far wall. KUNDSTDÜNGER was printed on each sack in bold red letters.

Tim felt the pellets in his pocket. There had been quite a lot on the ground outside the shed and he'd scooped them up carefully. They'd be good for the carp in the pond in the back garden. He felt pleased with himself as he turned into the driveway of Gustav Strasse Sieben. Heinz was polishing the khaki Volkswagen.

Tim reached into his pocket and brought out some pellets. 'Kunstdünger,' he said.

Heinz looked up and smiled. 'Kunstdünger?' He looked at the pellets and took one, rubbing it between his finger and thumb. He sniffed and then shook his head. 'Nein, this is not Kunstdünger.'

'Not Kunstdünger?' Tim was puzzled. 'But the sack had that printed on it, Heinz.'

'What sack?' Dad was walking down the path.

'At the Country Club, Dad. All the sacks had KUNSTDÜNGER printed on them.'

'This is not dünger,' said Heinz.

'What on earth is dünger?' Dad shook his head. What is all this?'

'Dünger is for feeding plants,' said Heinz.

'Dung! Dünger!' Tim smiled. 'It's the same as English.

'Well, not quite the same, Tim.' Dad smiled. 'Now, tell me what this is all about.'

'So.' Dad smiled at Tim. 'They nabbed Welch red-handed.

'Did the police get the whole gang?' asked Tim. 'Zeiger and the others?'

'I reckon so.' Dad smiled. 'Thanks to you, old son.' He nodded. 'The whole thing is extremely complex. But the sewer is the key; it led to all kinds of places, even to the DP camp where Kotsko lives.'

'Thank goodness he wasn't involved,' said Mum.

Dad nodded. 'I agree. Anyway, now we know why the cost of garden maintenance for the Country Club was so high. Welch was buying pellets to feed the fish with club funds and putting it in the books as... What's that word, Tim?'

'Kunstdunger, Dad. The kunst bit means it's not real dung; it's artificial.'

'Right.' Dad smiled. 'You're getting quite good at German, Tim. I think you have an ear for languages.

Anyway, back to Welch. None of the club committee members knew a thing about rhododendrons, especially mature trees like that, so no one had any idea he was fiddling, pretending to buy fertilizer for the rhododendrons.'

'He's a real wheeler-dealer, isn't he, Dad.'

Dad nodded. 'He is, Tim. Or rather, he was.' Dad stroked his bristly fair moustache. 'He was involved in the theft from the farms, too.'

'Will he go to prison, Dad?'

'Yes, Tim. No more wheeling and dealing for our Mr. Welch for a long, long time. But he's lucky he won't have to face a military court.'

'Why, Dad?'

'They stopped trying Control Commission personnel in military court a year ago. He'll face a civil court.' Dad shook his head. 'Jail is bad enough, but the military would have jailed him for years, and a military prison is not a nice place to be.'

'It's that poor woman I feel sorry for,' said Mum. 'She was mortified.'

'Shame,' said Dad. 'At least the authorities arranged for her and the boy to be sent home immediately. I understand they've gone to her mother's.'

Mum nodded. 'Somewhere in Essex. Good thing too I reckon. If the grandparents are anything like Muriel Welch, the boy will be better off.'

Dad nodded. 'You liked Muriel Welch, didn't you?'

Mum sighed. 'What a life she led. Now this.'

'What will happen to the fish, Dad?'

Tim frowned at Sarah; he'd wanted to ask that question. He was the one who'd helped catch the black market gang.

'They won't be sold on the black market, that's certain.' Dad smiled, his brown eyes sparkling. 'We'll harvest the mature fish, as Welch intended, just before Christmas.'

Tim nodded. At least the German boy would have time to catch a few before then. And there were other fish in the remaining ponds. He was sure that the boy was still visiting the ponds because of the trail through the grass. He frowned. Why was he bothered about the German boy?

'We'll keep the operation going next year,' said Dad. 'Do you remember the vet who treated Bits?'

'Captain McLaren?' said Mum.

'Right, Enid.' Dad nodded. 'He's been put in charge of the fish farm.' He turned to Inge. 'I understand carp is a Christmas meal for a lot of German families, Inge.'

'Ja. It is, mein Herr. If you get one I cook for you. But a live one, bitte.'

'Alive!' Sarah stared at Inge, her mouth open wide. 'You're not going to cook it alive?'

'Alive!' chimed in baby Jane.

Inge burst out laughing. Tears ran down her cheeks. She wiped them away with her apron. 'Nein! Nein! Sarah.' She shook her head. 'Aber, this fish must be put in fresh water for two or three days, to swim, to make clean inside. I will put in tub in basement.'

Chapter 26

BOMBER PILOT

Dad had set up the shelter as a darkroom. There was a single, dim, red bulb in the light socket. It cast an eerie glow around the room, creating soft-edged muted shadows on the concrete walls. The pungent smell of chemicals hung in the air.

'Have you finished the second film, Tim?'

'No, Dad. I still have one shot to take.'

'Well, how about taking it now, while I have the developing liquid ready?'

'Do I have to, Dad?'

'No. I suppose not.' Dad hung up a roll of developed film to dry from a clip suspended from the ceiling. 'I just thought that if you took it now we could develop that film too.' He rinsed his fingers and looked at Tim.

In the red glow of the lamp the white streak in Dad's hair stood out sharply. It was odd. Tim had noticed it before.

'Something special you want to take, is there?'

Tim nodded. 'Yes, Dad, and I don't have enough Baffs to buy another film.'

'Ah! I see. But I thought you wanted to use the flash powder.'

Tim remained silent. He did want to use the flash powder: It would be exciting setting the powder alight and taking a picture in the dark as it flashed brightly. But that wasn't it! He wanted to get a picture of the German boy; he didn't know why, but he did. Maybe it was because the boy had helped him that day at the pond.

Dad was still looking at him. 'What do you do with your pocket money, Tim? You should have enough for a film.'

Tim nodded. 'I do, Dad, but first I want to buy that book at the NAAFI.'

'Oh! You mean *Just William?*' Dad laughed. 'Good choice, Tim. I loved that book. Unfortunately, Richmal Crompton didn't start writing the William books until I was twelve or thirteen or I might have read more. I think the other one I read was *More William.*'

'That's the second one, Dad.' Tim nodded. 'But I'm also saving for Sarah's Christmas present.'

Dad smiled. 'I see. Not long to go now, only another two months.'

That was the problem. Time was running out, and every Saturday, when they went to the NAAFI, Tim saw Sarah staring at the stuffed Panda in the display case. Sarah had never had a Teddy Bear as she was born at the beginning of the war when toys like that were scarce. Tim knew she really wanted the Panda even though she didn't like to say. She was nine now and Mum said she was too old for stuffed toys, but Tim knew she wasn't. And now he too was beginning to stare at the Panda wondering if one day it would be gone before he had the money. Two weeks and he could get it.

'Well, we'd better clean up here then,' said Dad. You can open the door, Tim.'

'Okay, Dad.' Tim pushed down on the shiny brass lever and eased open the ship's door. It was heavy but swung open silently on the massive hinges. The daylight was bright after the dim red light in the shelter even though it was now late afternoon.

'Are we going to make those fireworks today, Dad, for Guy Fawkes Night? It's only a week away, well, a week and a half. Next Saturday is the first of November.'

'We could, some, anyway.' Major Athelstan smiled. 'I'm not guaranteeing they'll work, but I don't see why not.'

'Can we do it then, Dad?'

'Are Mum and the girls back from their walk with Bits?'

'I don't think so, Dad. Mum said she was going to pop in and see Mrs. Beecher for a cup of tea.'

'Right, then!' There was a twinkle in Dad's brown eyes. 'Let's make some fireworks. Give me a hand here and we'll get started.'

Ten minutes later they were busy at the bench under the basement window.

'A little more flash powder, Tim, but not too much or I won't be able to fold the straw. That's it. Good.' Dad folded the end of the paper drinking straw and tied it carefully with a piece of twine. Then he placed the straw on the bench. Black paper with a silvery white crust of dried saltpeter stuck out from the other end. 'The fuse looks good.' Dad smiled and then tapped the straw gently several times.

'Why did you do that, Dad?'

'I want to spread the powder evenly.' Carefully, Dad folded the straw first one way and then the other, an inch at a time, until it looked like a miniature concertina. 'Cut me a length of twine please, Tim. Six to eight inches long should do.' Dad nodded. 'Thanks. Now, I'll wrap that round to hold it together.'

Tim watched Dad's nail-less fingers carefully tie a knot in the string, his eyes focused in concentration. He could imagine Dad concentrating in that way when he'd been a bomb disposal officer. Dad hadn't looked up once while making the firework, not even to take the twine. No wonder he was so good with UXBs and high explosives. Last week he'd come home from a job in an underground mine where thousands of tons of explosives had been stored. When Mum had heard that some of the explosive was old and unstable she'd nearly had a fit. She hated those jobs. She said it was like the war again, never knowing if Dad might be killed. When Dad had gone missing in action in 1944 she had been devastated.

'There!' Dad snipped off the surplus twine and looked up. 'What do you think?'

'Super, Dad, absolutely wizard!'

'Right! Your turn, only this time we'll make a Catherine wheel. Then we can try a rocket; I've got some cardboard tubes for those; and then we can make some squibs and some bangers.'

Fifteen minutes later, as the light began to fade the bell rang at the front door. Muffled voices droned on for a while and then Tim heard the door closing. He wondered who it could have been. It wasn't Mum and the girls; if it had been then Bits would have come bounding down the stairs. Dad was so busy concentrating on the fireworks that Tim decided not to say anything, but he wondered who it was.

'There!' said Dad a while later. 'I reckon that's enough for today. Not a bad selection.'

Tim looked at the small pile of fireworks on the bench. There were six bangers, four rockets, eight jumping crackers, six squibs and three Catherine wheels. Dad said they'd make more next weekend. Guy Fawkes Night would be fun after all.

Dad started gathering the fireworks together. 'We'll keep everything in the darkroom, Tim. We don't want any mishaps when Mr. Kotsko stokes up the boiler in the morning.' Dad smiled. 'Give me a hand, and then we'll ask Inge to make us a cup of tea.'

Tim followed Dad into the shelter.

'Fireworks in that cupboard, Tim, powder here!' Dad nodded. 'A good afternoon's work, I'd say.'

'So, who came to visit, Enid?' Dad sipped his tea.

Mum was back from her walk with the girls and Bits.

'I don't know too much yet, Will. Inge was just starting to tell me when you two came up from the basement. As far as I know it was a man looking for his daughter.'

'Looking for his daughter?'

'Mm.' Mum nodded. 'He's just arrived from England. He was a prisoner of war.' Mum turned to Inge who was coming into the dining room from the kitchen. 'What was it that man told you, Inge?'

'He is prisoner since 1940, Frau Athelstan.' Inge placed a fresh plate of sandwiches on the table. 'He is Luftwaffe pilot in a bomber over London when he is shot down.'

'The Battle of Britain!' said Tim. 'I bet he was in the Battle of Britain. Was it September 1940, Inge?'

'Ja.' Inge nodded, 'September. He is prisoner in England und den Kanada.'

'Canada?' said Tim.

'Ja! Kanada. He like it there.' Inge sniffed and turned away. Tim saw her raise a corner of her apron to her eyes.

Mum got up. 'What's the matter, Inge?'

Inge started to sob. 'He went to find his family. They live in Buxtehude.'

'I know the place,' said Dad. 'It's fifteen, maybe twenty miles from here, across the Elbe.'

Inge nodded, still sobbing.

'What happened?' Mum put her arm around Inge's shoulders.

'His wife is dead nine months when he get there. Cholera. He think his boy is dead, too, taken for the Volks Sturm in 1945.'

'What's the Volks Sturm, Dad?' whispered Tim.

'Something like the Home Guard in England, Tim, only Hitler ordered boys as young as thirteen, and old men too, to put on Wermacht uniforms towards the end of the war. They were sent to man barricades in the streets. They were shot if they didn't. A lot of boys died.'

Tim shivered. He'd be thirteen soon. Hitler had been a monster. He listened as Inge continued:

'He is told his daughter go to Alstemarschen and he see a sign painted in the ruins in Hamburg, on a wall near the Reeperbahn.'

'What's the girl's name, Inge?' said Mum.

'Erica.' Inge dabbed her eyes with her apron.

Erica? Tim frowned. Erica? What was it...? Then he remembered: the message in the ruins. ERICA – ALSTEMARSCHEN. 'That was the sign we saw, Mum. In the ruins! Remember, just after I arrived?'

Mum nodded and reached into her pocket. As she pulled out a clean handkerchief her keys jangled on her belt. 'Here, Inge.' She thrust the cloth into Inge's hand and then turned and shook her head, putting a finger to her mouth. 'Let Inge go on.'

Inge sniffed into the handkerchief. 'I sorry I cry. I tell him we see no girl, but we have seen boy. He get excited.'

'Did he tell you the boy's name?' asked Dad.

'Ja.' Inge nodded, 'Otto. It is name of boy's Grossvater. He live in this house one time.'

'What?' Dad almost jumped out of his chair. 'This is his grandfather's house?'

Tim couldn't believe his ears. That would explain the combination lock on the shelter. And, if the boy who kept coming here with Bits was Otto, he'd been a soldier in the Volks Sturm. It didn't seem possible.

'This is the Grossvater house, Herr Athelstan. But he is dead.' Inge shook her head. 'He die in 1940, just before this man who came is shot down. This man is son. His

Mutter live here in war until 1944 when she is dead. The man know this. His bruder own house now.'

'Ah! So, Konrad Kiebel, the owner of this house must be the bomber pilot's brother, Inge!' Dad was rubbing the fingers of his hands. 'The children will be with him.'

'Ja. I say this.' Inge shook her head. 'Aber this man, his name is Werner, he is youngest child. Werner and Konrad fight.'

'Why?' asked Mum. 'Did he say?'

Inge nodded. She blew her nose loudly. Tim could see tears well up in her green eyes. 'Konrad hate the wife of Werner. She is student at Universität. Werner is student too. She is against Hitler.'

'I see.' Mum nodded.

Tim wondered if they'd known the old professor Dad knew from the university.

'Hm.' Dad was shaking his head slowly. 'But you know what they say: blood is thicker than water, and now with the war over… I wonder. Maybe this Konrad…'

Inge was shaking her head. 'The man, he has seen his brother. They still fight.'

'I see.' Dad turned to Tim. 'That boy, Tim, keep an eye out for him, will you.'

Tim nodded. He wondered if that would be fraternizing, but he wasn't going to ask.

Chapter 27

PHOTOGRAPH NUMBER EIGHT

Every day, on the way to and from school, Tim peered out of the bus as they passed the ruins by the river. But there was no sign of the boy or the old man. It was annoying. Where had they gone? When he got home from school, Tim spent as much time as possible peering through the binoculars in the attic. Where was the boy? Maybe his father, the bomber pilot, had found him. That had to be it. Inge said she hadn't seen the man again.

Then, a few days later, Dad made contact with Konrad Kiebel, the owner of Gustav Strasse Sieben.

'The man was totally disinterested in what happened to his brother or his family,' said Dad, at dinner that night. 'In fact he was more than just disinterested, he was downright hostile.' Dad shook his head, his lips pressed tightly together making his fair moustache bristle. 'He knew his sister-in-law was dead. He knew the family had been starving and needed help.' Dad thumped the table. 'The swine is obviously living well, despite the hardships of others and he didn't lift a finger to help his brother's family while he was a prisoner of war.'

'I can't believe it,' said Mum. She pushed a lock of light brown hair away from her eyes.

'There's more,' said Dad. 'I asked Heinz to ask Kiebel about the children, had he seen them? The swine had the audacity to smile while I was talking. He could understand English all right but refused to talk to me except with Heinz translating.' Dad sighed. 'Anyway, he said he'd seen the girl and sent her packing. Can you imagine that? I thought Heinz was going to hit him.'

'Oh, my…' Mum put her hand to her mouth, shaking her head.

Dad looked at Tim. 'By the way, you haven't seen that boy, have you, Tim?'

Tim shook his head. 'No, Dad, not since before the holiday. After we got back I thought I did, in a field. It was soon after we went back to school, before Herr Kiebel called here. It was one of the two days that Heinz drove me. But when I asked Heinz to turn round and go back I couldn't see him.' Tim looked out of the dining room window. Beyond the beechnut hedge were the fields, and beyond them the ruins. He was going to spend more time looking now. The trouble was, that since they'd put the clocks back, it was getting dark soon after he returned from school and he didn't have much time to use the binoculars. But when he went to the Country Club at the weekend he could look for the boy at the ponds. The large carp were still there; they hadn't been harvested yet. Tim felt his own anger rising. How could the boy's uncle not help him and his sister?

Dad was continuing: 'Heinz reckons Kiebel was a Nazi sympathizer. He probably still is.'

'Then why wasn't he brought in?' said Mum. 'I thought that was part of the de-Nazification process.'

'I checked.' Again Dad's lips set in a thin hard line. 'He was brought in. He was cleared. A lot of that happened.'

'How, Dad?' Tim looked at his father. 'How could someone who was a Nazi be found not to be a Nazi?'

'Probably bribery, Tim. Money can do a lot and Konrad Kiebel can certainly afford that.'

'But you said the Reichsmark was worthless, Dad.'

'So it is, Tim, but men like Kiebel know how to look after their money. He probably has money in Switzerland; he probably has a bank account, more than one, with American dollars.'

'I'm going to look for that boy,' said Sarah. 'I hope I see him.'

'Me too,' said baby Jane. 'I like boys.'

Tim couldn't help smiling despite himself. He wanted the boy to be found, but he hoped he'd be the one to find him. He'd seen him first. He'd rescued him from Reggie Welch. He'd rescued him from the farmer the morning they'd found Bits injured in the field. He'd rescued him from the man chasing them from the orchard. It wouldn't be fair if someone else found him, except Dad of course. He remembered the day the boy had rescued him from the pond. Should he tell Mum and Dad? It probably didn't matter about fraternizing any more, not the way Dad was talking now.

'I've told the MPs about the boy being seen around here,' said Dad, 'and about the girl visiting her uncle.

They've informed their counterparts in the local police. They've started a search for the father, too. That shouldn't take long, a returning P.O.W.'

Tim was silent. He knew that if the boy saw the Military Police and the German police he'd run. He not only poached rabbits and fish, but he was stealing, too; he had to be. He shut his eyes. He wouldn't tell Mum and Dad yet. He'd find the boy.

Tim got out of bed and crossed the room on tiptoe. He shivered. The house was incredibly warm from the central heating and he could feel waves of heat rising from the radiator beneath his window, but the bare fields looked cold and grey in the pale, early morning November light. The sky was clear, brightening by the minute as the sun crept up from beneath the horizon.

Every day for the past week he'd been up early, standing at the window, searching the fields for signs of movement. The harvest was long in, but one afternoon he was with Heinz in the Volkswagen when they'd seen a crowd of people in a field. Most of them had crude, long wooden rakes.

'What are they doing?' he asked Heinz.

'Gathering…' Heinz paused. 'In German we say 'korn'.'

'Corn? We say that too, Heinz.' Tim nodded. 'But why are they raking' He remembered seeing the corn being cut and stacked and taken in a few days before.

'It is nachlese.' Heinz shook his head. 'I don't know this in English. It is the pieces that drop.'

'You mean they're raking up the grains that dropped?'

'Ja. They boil it and make...' Once more Heinz shook his head. 'It is like your father has for breakfast.'

'Porridge, Heinz. You must mean porridge.' Tim looked back at the crowds in the field. There couldn't be much grain on the ground, and with all these people no one would get much. It was then that he'd thought of the boy. 'Heinz! Stop!'

'What is it?'

'Can you go back a bit, Heinz? I want to look.'

The driver reversed slowly back up the road, but if the boy had been around he was not in the crowd now.

As Tim stood at the window he thought about that afternoon before the boy's father had called at the house. If the boy had been gleaning fallen husks of corn then he probably searched the fields for other leftovers. Late last week the farmer nearby had harvested the turnips. The field was full of women, most of them on their knees digging with their hands. He'd seen no one in the turnip field since then, but knowing the boy, Tim thought he'd see him one day. Then there were the snares. Tim hadn't seen any rabbits lately, it was getting too cold, but, on the weekend, he'd found snares hidden behind the beechnut hedge. He didn't think the boy would leave them there, not unless he was with his dad.

Movement behind the hedge caught Tim's eye. Someone was there, moving slowly, furtively. Drat it! He wasn't dressed yet. The movement stopped. Was it the boy? Was he collecting his snares?

Hurriedly, Tim stripped off his pyjamas and pulled on his vest and shirt. While he pulled on his trousers he looked for his socks. Where were they? It would be easier with the light on but then the boy would see it and know someone was up. He'd probably run off. Ah! There they were.

As he pulled his jersey over his head he moved back to the window. It was getting lighter. The sun would be up soon, a pale wintry sun but enough to give him away if he wasn't careful. Then, further along the hedge this time, he saw movement again. Tim reached for the camera on top of his bureau. It might be light enough soon to get a photo. No, that was stupid. If he was going to catch the boy, and he knew he could outrun him, he wouldn't have time for that. Just the same… He slung the camera strap over his head.

Tim crept silently down the path from the kitchen door. It was bitterly cold outside after the warmth of the house and he wished he'd put on more clothes. The sky was getting lighter by the minute. He didn't want to waste time, but he couldn't go any faster without making noise. He passed the brick pond and the greenhouse and then froze. The beechnut hedge was about twenty feet away, bare of leaves. The boy was moving quickly to the right. Tim could see him quite clearly, silhouetted against the rising sun. His hair was longer now. He let the boy move on and then followed silently along the inside of the hedge until he came to the gap that led into the field. Carefully he eased through. Now he wished he'd brought Bits, but it was too late: Bits was in the basement, snug and warm. Tim shivered.

The boy had two snares in his right hand. The long wooden pegs with their sharp ends dangled from the tarnished brass wire and swung back and forth as he ran. The bag slung over his shoulder was bulging, obviously heavy. He wore a baggy pair of cutoff black trousers, tied round his waist with a rope; and he had a sort of pullover, tucked at the waist inside the trousers, that looked like it was made from a sack. His feet were bare. He must be frozen! But worse, he was getting away, running along the side of the potato field by the hedge.

Tim broke into a run. He wanted to catch up with the boy as quickly as possible. The ground was rough and uneven with clods of frozen earth making it difficult to maintain a steady pace. And the boy was moving fast, faster than Tim had anticipated. He had to strain to gain on him.

The boy slipped through a gap in the hedge into the cabbage field. It was then that Tim saw the other figure. It was the tall thin man; the man who had beaten Bits; the man watching Zeiger at the pond. Where had he come from? Was he a poacher? The man was so intent on watching the boy that he hadn't seen Tim yet. He stood on the opposite side of the hedge from the boy, the side Tim was on. His right hand slowly, rhythmically slapped a stick against his leg. Then he started to run along the side of the hedge, his long legs carrying him quickly over the ground. Tim didn't know what to do. He looked back over his shoulder; Gustav Strasse Sieben was away in the distance; it was incredible how far he'd come! He looked back across the field. The man was now on the other side of the hedge. How had he done that? There must be another gap.

Tim ran along the hedge. He couldn't see the boy or the man now. Should he go on? Then he heard a cry of pain. It was the boy. He'd been caught. He heard a dull thud and another cry of pain. Why hadn't he brought Bits?

'Wo ist der Grossvater?' The man's voice was menacing. 'Wo – ist – der – Grossvater?'

After each word Tim heard a thud followed by a muted cry. Was the man kicking the boy? Tim crouched down and slowly and silently crept along the side of the short hedge.

'Ich weiss nicht. Ich weiss nicht.' The boy was sobbing uncontrollably, gasping for breath. 'Ich weiss nicht.'

There was a whistling sound and another cry of pain. Tim knew that sound. The man was beating the boy with the stick. Tim couldn't stand it. He looked round and spotted four large stones each about the size of a large potato. He gathered them quietly and, crouching low made his way along the hedge until he was behind the man.

Tim saw the arm rise high above the hedge, the stick grasped in a bony hand. The armpit of the man's coat was torn, as was the shirt beneath, revealing very white skin. The man's back was towards him. Tim stood up slowly. As the arm swung down Tim threw a stone, putting all his strength behind it.

'Ah!' The man dropped to his knees, holding the back of his head. 'Ah!' The second stone hit in almost the same place.

The boy was half crouched, staring first at the man and then Tim. There were two ugly welts on his face. His bag was beside him, yellow turnips spilled on the ground; but the snares were still in his hand. As the man struggled to get up the boy struck him with the sharpened pegs; he was in a frenzy sobbing and crying each time he brought the snares down on the man's head. But suddenly the man reached up and grabbed the wire. He was staggering but getting to his feet.

Tim threw another stone. It missed and the man turned towards him. His face was pale, distorted with rage, anger making the short scar on his right cheek stand out red against the livid skin. Above the scar his right eye half closed and then opened involuntarily; flecks of spittle bubbled from the side of his mouth.

'Argh!' He ran at the hedge, reaching for Tim, but the hedge was too thick. His arm was raised, his hand gripping the stick so tightly that the knuckles stood out hard and white.

For a moment, Tim stood rooted to the spot. Then he threw the last stone. It was rough and jagged. As it left his hand it seemed to glide slowly through the air, taking an age to reach its mark. And it was almost as if the man was moving in slow motion too, watching the rock sail towards him, his arm raised high revealing a tattoo on the skin showing through the hole in his torn clothing. Then the jagged stone struck him on the left temple. His jaw sagged and he fell to the ground, motionless, eyes staring up at the sky. Blood trickled from the wound in his temple onto the hard ground.

The boy looked down, then up at Tim. 'Er ist tot!'

Tim stared over the hedge. He'd killed him. He'd killed somebody! His heart raced and he felt icy cold. His legs were shaking uncontrollably and he thought he was going to be sick. Then he saw the man's chest rising and falling slowly. He wasn't dead.

The boy was staring down at the man too, as if unable to take his eyes off him. He stepped back, his eyes wide with fear. Then he stared at Tim, tears streaming down his cheeks.

Tim looked for a way through the hedge. There were no gaps in sight and it was too thick to climb through. He fumbled for the camera under his coat but it was too late. The boy picked up his bag and, turning, started to run. Then he turned quickly to wave.

'Otto!' Tim shouted. 'Otto!'

The boy's mouth dropped open. His shoulders drooped and he let out a piercing wail, tears streaming down his bloodied face. Then, as Tim pulled out the camera he turned again and ran.

The man lay on the ground, moaning. His eyes were now closed but his breathing was becoming noisy. Tim held the camera to his chest and looked into the viewfinder. The hedge hid the man's legs but his head and chest were framed in the small rectangle of glass.

Chapter 28

FRITZ! BIST DU ES?

'Is this the place, Tim?'

'I'm pretty sure it is, Dad.'

Tim couldn't believe it. Snow had started to cover the ground, yet it seemed as if only a few minutes had passed since he'd raced home and wakened Mum and Dad. Inge had shrieked in fright when he'd rushed in through the kitchen door. And Heinz had stared in disbelief as he'd raced up the stairs.

Now they were here in the field: Dad, Heinz, himself and Bits. But the man was gone. Bits was sniffing around excitedly, his short stubby tail pointing straight up.

Then Tim saw the turnips. They were almost covered by snow. The bag was gone, but in his haste to get away the boy hadn't picked up the spilled food.

'This is the place, Dad.' Tim pointed. 'Look! The boy had those turnips in his bag. They spilled out when the man threw him to the ground. And there!' Tim pointed again, 'there's the stick he was hitting him with and…' He bent down. 'This is one of the stones I threw.'

Dad took the stone, brushing off the snow. He turned it over. 'Hm. You're right, son. There are traces of blood on it. You really did hurt him.'

Tim shivered. It was cold here in the field, and the snow that at first had fallen in large fluffy flakes was now smaller, driven by a biting wind. But more than that, he felt again the icy chill that gripped him when he saw the man on the ground and thought he had killed him. He shook himself to get rid of that horrible feeling.

Bits was whining, straining on the leash. Tim looked at him. Heinz was having quite a job holding Bits back as the dog pulled in the direction of the ruins.

'He can smell the boy, Dad. He wants to follow him.'

Dad nodded, turning his back to the wind. 'I know, Tim, but not in this blizzard. None of us is dressed for this and soon we'll not be able to see a foot in front of our faces.' He leaned down and scratched Bits between the ears. 'Come on! Let's get back to the house!'

Tim hesitated, imagining the boy struggling across the fields with bare feet, and with only the sack to keep him warm against the driving snow. But maybe he'd found shelter. Maybe he'd already got to the ruins; Tim was sure that's where he lived.

'Tim! Come on, lad!' Dad's right hand rested on his shoulder. 'We must get home. Heinz! I'll take Bits.' He held out his left hand.

Bits looked up as Dad tugged on the leash; his dark eyes were troubled and his brow, covered in short dark brown hair was creased in a worried frown. He whined and looked back across the field.

Tim heard Dad's quiet, soothing voice. 'Don't worry Bits. We'll find him.' Dad pulled gently on the lead. 'Later. We'll find him.'

Bits lowered his head and started to walk slowly towards the house.

The pungent smell of the photographic chemicals filled Tim's nose. He breathed in deeply. He liked it. The red light glowed, highlighting the streak in Dad's hair as he bent over the shallow tray on the bench. His hands were shaking. Tim hadn't seen Dad like this since he came home from the war.

'Describe him again, Tim.'

'But I've told you at least ten times, Dad.'

Dad turned. He was finished and he hung up the roll of film to dry. 'Again, son, please. I have to be sure.'

'But you'll see when you make the print, Dad.'

Dad rubbed the ends of the fingers on his right hand with his left. In the silence of the shelter it sounded like paper being rubbed on paper. 'Again please, son.' He turned back to the bench and leaned forward, his hands resting on the bare wooden top.

Tim sighed. 'Well, he's tall; taller than Heinz. And he's thin. He's got bony hands.'

'And he carried that stick?'

'Yes, Dad, in his right hand; and he kept slapping it against his leg.' In his mind Tim could see the evil face. 'And he has a scar under his right eye and... oh, yes, I almost forgot, Dad: his coat and his shirt were torn and in his armpit he had a tattoo.'

Dad whirled round. In the red glow of the darkroom his face was changed, his teeth bared as if in agony, the skin stretched tautly over his cheekbones. His had a wild look and his voice was strange, raw and gasping. 'It's him, Tim. I know it's him.'

The photograph lay on the table. The Military Police captain made a note in his book. 'Just to confirm this, Tim. You say you've seen this man twice before?'

Tim nodded. If he'd only known before what the SS man looked like. But Dad had never described him, had never mentioned the mannerism with the stick. If he had Tim could have told him. And the man had never whistled that tune Mum had told him about.

'Was that a yes, Tim?' The captain asked.

'Yes, sir, in the potato field, shortly after I came here. He was the man who almost killed Bits.'

'That was in May?'

'Yes, Captain.' Mum nodded. 'Tim arrived just before the Whitsun holiday.'

'Right.' The policeman smiled at Tim. 'And then you saw him again.'

Tim nodded. 'I didn't realize it was him at the time.' He shivered. No wonder he'd felt scared. Even though he didn't know who the man was there was something evil about him. 'I was down at the ponds, at the Country Club. The SS man was watching Zeiger feed the carp.'

The captain shook his head. 'There's something about that Welch character and Zeiger that has me puzzled.'

Dad was staring out of the window. He'd been silent during most of the interview, but when the military police officer mentioned Welch he nodded slowly.

'And then this time, Tim.' The policemen looked across the table.

'This is the third time, sir.'

'Right. Thank you, Tim. You've been most helpful.' The officer picked up the photograph and put it in his book. He turned to Dad. 'There's no doubt in your mind, Major, that this is Ober Leutnant Arnhaust?'

'None. None at all.' Dad shook his head and stared down at his hands. 'That man's evil face has haunted me for over two years. And it will continue to haunt me until we catch him and bring him to trial.' He looked up, his brown eyes narrowed. His voice was barely above a whisper. 'Catch the swine!'

Mum reached out and gently took Dad's right hand in hers.

The policeman stood up. 'We'll get him, sir. He has to be hiding close to here. We'll get him. But in the meantime, take care.'

Dad shook his head. 'Take care?' He laughed, a short, sharp shallow sound. 'I shudder to think what could have happened. My family...here.'

'Yes sir.' The policeman looked grim. 'I know what you're thinking. But I think we can be fairly sure that he has no idea you live here. Welch didn't tell him, that's certain; he probably hasn't met him. And even if he did Welch probably had no idea he was SS. I don't think he knows the connection. If he had known, I agree, it could have been disastrous.' He made a note in his book. 'In any event, I'll follow up on that immediately.'

Tim shuddered as he thought of all the times he'd been on his own, of the times by the ponds, in the field. If the Nazi officer had known he was Dad's son and that Dad was so close by! He shook his head. Then he remembered what Mum had said about hiding in a place people least expected. That's what the SS officer had done! He'd hidden near the British officers! Who would look there?

The Military Police captain was talking to Mum. 'I'll be leaving Corporal Rogers here, Mrs. Athelstan, until I can send the two-man detail over. They'll be changed every twelve hours.' He turned to Dad. 'Rest assured, Major, I'll move heaven and earth to catch this one.'

'Thank you, Captain.'

As the Military Police officer turned to leave, the corporal knocked on the dining room door and looked in. 'Someone coming up the path, sir, looks foreign to me.'

There was a rap on the front door.

The captain held up his hand as Dad rose from the table. 'I'll get it, sir. Come with me, Rogers.' The policemen strode purposefully into the hall. Tim heard the front door open and then a surprised voice:

'Oh! I wasn't expecting the military police! You're not…? No, I see you are a captain. I'm looking for Major Athelstan.' The man's English was good but with a clipped Germanic sound and a strange drawl.

'And you are?' asked the MP officer.

'Werner Kiebel,' said the voice. 'I called here some weeks ago and…'

Bits had pricked up his ears and started to bark excitedly. His nails scrabbled on the polished wooden floor as he scrambled to get up. Then he bounded out of the room.

'Fritz! Bist du es?' The man at the door sounded excited. 'Bist du es, werlich, Fritz?'

Chapter 29

FLAMES IN THE RUINS

The Volkswagen purred along the snow-covered road. Heinz leaned forward, hunched over the wheel, peering through the windshield as the wipers shuddered slowly back and forth across the glass. Dad didn't trust his own driving in these wintry conditions so he didn't want to bring the Opal, although everyone would have been much more comfortable, including Fritz. And Dad had also been worried that Bits, as he still called him, in his obvious excitement might tear the leather upholstery in the Opal.

'No wonder he answered so readily to that name,' Tim heard Dad say from the back seat. 'Bits, Fritz.' Dad laughed. 'Oh, all right you silly old dog.'

Tim could hear Bits slobbery licks. Dad laughed again, as did Herr Kiebel. The two men seemed to be getting along really well. It was strange in a way. Tim peered through the windshield; it was difficult to see through the driving snow. He hoped he could find the stubby road leading into the ruins. The wipers staggered on, back and forth, juddering at times in their effort to keep the glass clear. Heinz grasped the wheel, leaning further forward. It was getting dark.

'It's got to be near here, Heinz.' Tim peered out of the side window, thinking about what had happened since Herr Kiebel had arrived.

At one point he thought they might not come to find the boy. It would have been his fault. The Military Police captain had already left when Tim remembered something he'd forgotten in all the excitement. Everyone had been so keen on the description of the Nazi officer that they hadn't asked if he'd said anything. Then, shortly after Herr Kiebel had arrived and was asking about his son, Otto, Tim had suddenly remembered the SS man's words as he hit the boy. He thought Herr Kiebel would want to know.

'He kept asking Otto about his grandfather.' Tim had looked across the table at the Luftwaffe bomber pilot. Her Kiebel was quite thin, but his face and hands were deeply tanned and weathered from working in the fields in Canada where he'd been sent as a prisoner of war. Tim realized that was how he got the drawl.

'His grandfather?' Herr Kiebel stared at Tim. 'I don't understand.'

Tim nodded. 'I know it was his grandfather because that's a word I learned a long time ago from Inge.'

'But Otto no longer has a grandfather,' said Herr Kiebel, the excitement leaving his voice. 'My father died in 1940, just before I was shot down and taken prisoner.' He shook his head. 'And I heard from Gerda, my wife that is, in one of the few letters that reached me before she died that her father died in 1943. This boy cannot be Otto.'

He looked so disappointed that Tim wished he hadn't said anything.

'Major Athelstan.' Herr Kiebel turned to Dad. 'I am sorry I bothered you.' He started to rise.

Tim couldn't believe it. 'But, sir, it's got to be Otto! You should have seen his face when I shouted his name; his mouth fell open he was so surprised.' Tim hurried on. 'And then there's Bits... I mean Fritz. Fritz was with Otto that day, when we found him'

'Of course this is true!' Herr Kiebel nodded, his eyes beginning to shine again. 'I think... I hope you are right. But I don't understand about the grandfather.'

Dad had been listening intently, saying nothing. Suddenly he went deathly pale. 'Say that again, Herr Kiebel. Please.'

Herr Kiebel shook his head. 'I don't understand,' he said. 'You mean about the grandfather?'

Dad nodded. *The grandfather!*' He paused. *The grandfather!* Tim, can you remember exactly what the SS man said? It's important. It's so important I can hardly believe it might be possible.'

Tim looked at his father. Dad was staring at him, a strange light in his brown eyes, almost pleading. Then he saw Herr Kiebel look down at Dad's hands as he rubbed the nail-less ends, first one hand then the other. What was so important? He had to think. He shut his eyes and imagined himself back behind the hedge. He heard the whistle of the stick slicing through the cold morning air, once, twice, three times, four times:

'Wo... ist... der... Grossvater?' He heard the words ringing in his head. He opened his eyes.

'Wo ist der Grossvater. He said Wo ist der Grossvater?'

'Ah.' Herr Kiebel was nodding. 'This is strange. He was asking about 'a grandfather' but...'

'I know.' Dad interrupted. 'It's *The Grandfather*. He's after Der Grossvater, the message carrier.' He turned to Tim. 'You've heard The Grandfather's voice, Tim.'

'I have, Dad?' What was Dad going on about now?

'The voice on the wireless, Tim; the voice you heard on the crystal set you made during the war. The code! Remember when you heard my name?' Dad started to sing:

'Tom Pearce, Tom Pearce, lend me your grey mare. All along, down along, out along lea...'

Dad's voice was like Grandpa George's when he'd sung that song in the kitchen at Medbury, three long years ago. But it wasn't Grandpa George's voice that Dad was talking about; it was the foreign voice that sang the song in code and that Tim had heard on his crystal set. It was the coded message sent over the radio from Europe during the war, telling listeners that men who were missing in action, or who had escaped, were alive and safe.

'Tom Pearce, Tom Pearce lend me your grey mare... With Will Athelstan, Tom Morse, David Hall ....' The names of the men who were free were inserted into the song. And Tim had heard Dad's name, *Will Athelstan,* on that winter night just before Christmas 1944.

'The Grandfather,' said Dad. 'We must find him!' Dad was looking at Herr Kiebel. 'The Professor, The

Grandfather as he was called, is a prime witness against SS Ober Leutnant Arnhaust.'

'The Professor?' Herr Kiebel sounded troubled. 'What is his name, Major?'

Tim turned in his seat. Dad was shaking his head. 'We never knew him by name; that would have been too dangerous. He was always called The Grandfather.' In the fading light Dad's face looked grim. 'Arnhaust will kill him if he finds him. He'll torture him and then kill him, and anyone with him! Your boy, Kiebel! Oh, my... Tim! Can you find this place?'

Tim nodded. He had to!

The car jolted and swayed as it hit a pothole. Tim's head hit the window and he winced with pain. He blinked and then shouted:

'There it is, Heinz. Over there!'

The Volkswagen slid to the right as Heinz braked. Then it stopped with a slight bump. The cleared stub of road was behind them on the right. Tim had only just seen it as the headlights of the little car swept past the narrow entrance. A blanket of snow covered the ruins, hiding the jagged piles of broken brick and concrete, giving everything a soft rounded look.

'Leave the car here, Heinz,' said Dad quietly.

'Ja, mein Herr.' Heinz switched off the engine. 'I leave the side lights on so we can find him.'

Tim smiled to himself. It was funny how Heinz always referred to the car in this way. It was the German grammar of course. As Tim stepped out of the car Bits tried to follow.

'Hold on, Bits.' Dad pushed the seat forward and climbed out of the back. 'Hm.' Dad was looking down the short stub of road between the ruins. 'Someone has been here fairly recently.'

Tim saw footprints in the snow, large prints in a single line leading up into the ruins.

'Ah! Mein Gott!' Herr Kiebel forced his way out of the car and pushed forward. He was starting to run when Dad grabbed his arm.

'I know what you are thinking,' Dad said, 'but I suggest we proceed carefully and quietly.'

Herr Kiebel nodded. 'You are right.' He held out his left hand. 'I will take Fritz, please.'

'Right!' Dad handed him the leash. 'Let's go.'

It was difficult climbing the mountain of rubble at the end of the road. The snow hid cracks and crevices and Tim found his foot stuck several times. Once he almost lost a boot. It was slippery in places, too. But Bits seemed to have no difficulty and almost pulled Mr. Kiebel after him; they had already reached the top and he and Bits were outlined against the falling snow by a reddish-glow. Mr. Kiebel was pointing, and as Tim heaved himself over the top he saw flames in the ruins below.

'Dad! Look!' he whispered.

It wasn't an open fire but a short metal chimney sticking out of the ground at an angle. The metal glowed red as flames flickered from the jagged opening, sending showers of sparks into the cold night air to die as they landed in the snow.

Dad held up a hand. 'Shush!'

They moved forward quietly and deliberately.

They were close to the chimney when Dad stopped suddenly, motionless and tense. Bits was straining on his leash, alternately whining and growling deep in his throat. Tim felt a shiver down his spine; he looked at his father. In the yellow-red glow of the flames Dad's face was drawn and tense, the white streak through his hair highlighted. He leaned forward, head to one side. Heinz was listening too, staring at Dad. Then Tim heard the sound; it was faint, but someone was whistling. Dad's hands were trembling, shaking, and he closed his eyes, hanging his head, breathing in slowly and deeply. As Heinz rested his hand on Dad's shoulder the whistling stopped.

The anguished cry rising from the ground beneath his feet shook Tim out of his reverie. Mum had said the SS officer always whistled that tune before he started to torture someone. Ober Fuhrer Arnhaust was here! Tim started to run.

'Tim!' Dad's voice was sharpened by the icy cold of the night air. 'Tim!'

Then Bits raced past Tim and seemed to disappear into the ground. As Tim found the opening, he heard Bits' deep-throated growl and a cry of rage. Then he heard the boy's voice:

'Frital Frital Bist du es? Bist du es, wirllch!'

Mr. Kiebel pushed past Tim.

Chapter 30
SILENT NIGHT

Tim would never forget that night. As he lay in bed he recalled every image. Every detail was marked indelibly in his mind: the small iron stove, a witch-furnace on four legs in the corner; an oil lamp casting a yellow glow; The Grandfather seated on an old car seat, bound with rope, his face smeared with blood; the boy at the old man's feet, crying, the welts on his cheeks now deep purple bruises; the SS Ober Leutnant, his head swathed in a makeshift bandage, the eye above the scar twitching uncontrollably. Tim, like Dad, would never be able to forget that man.

And then, as Herr Kiebel shouted, Bits jumped. He was well fed now, not starved and weak as he had been that early morning in the field long ago. The SS officer's arm was raised as he prepared to strike The Grandfather. And Tim could see the tattoo. In his left hand Ober Leutnant Arnhaust held a knife, the blade silver-gold in the yellow light of the oil lamp. Bits didn't go for the raised arm; his jaws locked onto the man's left wrist.

'Argh!' The SS officer cried out in pain and anger as the knife fell to the floor.

At the same time Tim saw Heinz leap forward, grasp the stick and wrestle the man to the ground.

'Otto?' There was uncertainty in Herr Kiebel's voice as he dropped to the ground and pulled the boy to him.

'Nein, Vater. Nicht Otto.' The boy was sobbing, reaching up. 'Ich bin Erica.'

Erica! As Tim snuggled down into bed he smiled to himself. Erica! At first he hadn't realized what he was hearing. Then he remembered the painted sign in the ruins and Inge telling them that Herr Kiebel had a daughter, Erica.

The scene in the basement in the ruins returned once more. This time the sights and sounds went round and round in his head:

Herr Kiebel's surprised voice. 'Professor Hoing?'

Dad kneeling at the old man's feet. 'Grossvater. Grossvater. Ich bin Major Athelstan.'

The old man nodding and smiling, and then in a weak voice singing: 'Will Athelstan, Tom Morse, David Hall...' The coded song from Christmas 1944 that Tim had picked up on the crystal set.

And then he saw Herr Kiebel, tears streaming down his face, rocking back and forth, hugging his daughter. And Erica, reaching out towards Tim, holding his hand tightly as he knelt beside her father. Her dark hair, longer now, fell across her forehead, above her deep blue eyes. How could he have mistaken her for a boy?

And now it was Christmas night. And Dad was happy. Tim could hear the drone of voices downstairs and the occasional loud burst of laughter. Herr Kiebel had a pleasant low, rolling laugh. Tim wondered if Erica and Sarah were asleep yet, probably not. He sighed. It had been a super Christmas. Sarah had been so surprised when she opened the parcel and saw the Panda. And he'd enjoyed the singing at St. Thomas à Beckett church in Hamburg. Erica had sung the words of Silent Night in German. And then, when they returned to Gustav Strasse Sieben, they had goose, and carp prepared by Inge. As they finished the Christmas pudding Dad raised his right hand, a smile on his face. He looked at Mum.

'Let us say grace,' he said.

'Oh, no, Will. You're not.' Mum shook her head. 'Not that silly old thing!'

Dad nodded. 'If my Dad can say it then so may I.' He cleared his throat and looked round the table:

'We thank the Lord for what we've had. If there was more we would be glad. But as the times are very bad, we thank the Lord for what we've had.'

Mum sighed. 'I suppose you're right, Will. The times are bad. But we are very lucky, very, very lucky indeed.'

Tim snuggled into the pillow. Erica looked very pretty in the new clothes Mum had got for her from Mrs. Beecher. She would no longer have to wear old boys' clothes and would no longer need to cut her hair short. That's how she'd stayed out of trouble, of course, hair cropped short, with everyone thinking she was a boy. Tim sighed. He wondered when they'd find Otto. He was alive, or had been, at the end of the war. Tim shook his head. Otto was only a year older than he was when he'd been captured and made a prisoner of war. He'd been released. Dad had found that out.

In the hall downstairs the telephone rang shrilly. The laughing stopped and Tim heard the living room door open. Dad's voice was too low to make out what he was saying, but he wondered who would call on Christmas night. He started to doze.

A little while later Tim's door opened slowly.

'Are you asleep, Tim?' It was Dad.

'No, Dad.' Tim stifled a yawn and opened his eyes.

'Good.' Dad's shadowy shape approached the bed. 'I just wanted to thank you again, old chap.' Tim felt Dad's nail-less fingers on his. 'I'm so pleased that you are here.'

Tim felt warm and cozy. It was like old times, well almost. 'Is it alright if I like Erica, Dad?'

Dad chuckled. 'Of course, Tim, I like her father. In fact I like him a lot.'

Tim smiled to himself and then said: 'It's like Inge said, Dad.'

'What's that, Tim? What did Inge say?'

Tim was silent for a moment. He'd better not say about the clothes, not yet, not until they were back in England. 'She said we're all the same, Dad. English, French, Canadians, Americans, Germans.'

'Well, there's some truth in that, Tim. But a lot of people wouldn't agree at all.' Dad squeezed his hand. 'It's a nice thought. You hold on to it. Anyway, that call was from the MPs.'

'Was it about the SS officer, Dad?'

'Yes, and about Welch and Zeiger.'

'Did Mr. Welch know Ober Leutnant Arnhaust?'

'No, son' Dad shook his head. 'As much as I dislike Welch he had nothing to do with Arnhaust, and neither did Zeiger. But the farmer behind us did. He's hidden several wanted war criminals in his attic over the past two years. Ober Leutnant Arnhaust was there, waiting for safe passage out of Germany.'

Tim felt cold, remembering the day he and Erica had been scrumping, when he'd run back to the orchard to get his towel and shirt. He'd passed the farmhouse, not close, but he was near. Dad was continuing:

'On one of the few occasions when he left hiding he saw Professor Hoing with Erica. At the time a Military Police patrol was in the area and stopped nearby. Arnhaust thought they were after him.'

'They weren't, Dad?'

'No, Tim, but by the time he realized that, The Grandfather had disappeared. What he also didn't know was that the old man had lost his memory.'

'But the professor sang the song, Dad. He remembered you and Sergeant Morse.'

'That's the most incredible thing, Tim. When Arnhaust followed Erica's footprints in the snow and found her and The Grandfather in the ruins, and started torturing the old man, gradually, through the pain his memory started to return. And when we arrived...'

'He remembered everything, Dad?'

'That's right, son.'

'And if the Ober Leutnant hadn't gone there he could have escaped and never have faced trial.'

'Right, Tim. Anyway,' Dad continued, 'the MPs have arrested the farmer.'

'Super, Dad, but what about Mr. Welch? What about Zeiger?'

'Ah, ha!' Dad was laughing quietly. 'I shouldn't laugh, but this will surprise you. It surprised me. Zeiger was the black market chief in this area. Who would suspect a driver?'

'The chief, Dad?' Now Tim understood. 'No wonder Mr. Welch had never met the top man, or thought he hadn't. No wonder Zeiger said the chief was afraid of a trap and wouldn't meet Mr. Welch. It was him; Zeiger was the top man.'

'Right, son.' Dad continued: 'Welch had no idea Zeiger was in any way connected with the top people in the black market; he thought he was just part of the black market set up. But he did discover that Zeiger was using him in his position in Supplies Distribution. His greed was his downfall and he decided to turn the tables. Thanks to you he was caught.'

Dad ruffled Tim's hair. 'So, there it is. This will be a Christmas you won't forget, I'll bet.'

Tim sighed. 'Never, Dad! Never!'

THE END

Glossary

GERMAN WORDS AND PHRASES

The following glossary and notes are given to assist readers if necessary. However, the context in which German words and phrases are used makes the sense clear.

German	English	German	English
aber	but	Ja	Yes
Amiesen	ants	junge	young
Bist du	Are you	Kanada	Canada
Bist due s?	Is it you?	Karpfen	Carp
Bitte	please	Kitzeln	tickle
Blödmann	silly man	Korn	corn
Bruder	brother	Kügelchen	pellet
Danke	Thank you	Kundstdunger	fertilizer
dann	then	mein, meine	my
das ist gut	that is good	Mein Gott	My God
das ist nicht	that's not	mein Herr	sir
das ist wahr	that is true	Mönchs-kloster	monastery
der, die, das	the	mutter	mother
dieb	thief	nachlese	gleanings
dünger	dung, manure	nein	no

German	English	German	English
ein, eine	a	nicht wahr	isn't it
er ist tot	he is dead	Ober Leutnant	Lieutenant
Frau	Mrs.	Pille	pill
Freunden	friend (f)	Platz!	Stay!
Grossmutter	grandmother	Reichsmark	money
Grossvater	grandfather	schwachkopf	simpleton
gut	good	Schweinehund	rotter, swine
haferbrei	porridge	sieben	seven
haferflockan	oat flakes	Sitz!	Sit!
Halt!	Stop!	Strasse	street
hausboot	houseboat	und	and
Herr	Mr.	universität	university
Ich bin	I am	Vater	father
Ich weiss nicht	I don't know	Volks Sturm	Home Guard
Idiot	Idiot	werlich	truly
Ist alles in odnung?	Is everything alright?	wild	wild
		Wilddieb	poacher
Ist gut	It's good	wo ist	where is

Place Names

Alstemarschen: A fictitious suburb west of Hamburg.

Buxtehude: A real city south of the Elbe river.

Cuxhaven: A German port on the North Sea.

Hamburg: A city founded one thousand years ago by the great Emperor Charlemagne. Hamburg is the largest port in Germany. It lies inland on the river Elbe. Half of the city was destroyed by bombs in World War II.

Lübeck:	A city north-east of Hamburg near the Baltic.
Travermünde:	A seaside resort on the Baltic Sea.